THE FRENCH LIST

ALSO AVAILABLE

'A Very Fine Gift'
*and Other Writings on **Theory***

'The "Scandal" of Marxism'
*and Other Writings on **Politics***

'Simply a Particular Contemporary'
Interviews, 1970–79

Signs and Images
*Writings on **Art**, **Cinema** and **Photography***

'Masculine, Feminine, Neuter'
and Other Writings
on **Literature**

Roland Barthes

Essays and Interviews, Volume **3**

TRANSLATION AND
EDITORIAL COMMENTS
BY **CHRIS TURNER**

LONDON NEW YORK CALCUTTA

www.bibliofrance.in

The work is published with the support of the Publication Assistance Programmes of the Institut français

Seagull Books, 2023

Compiled from Roland Barthes, *Oeuvres complètes* (Éditions du Seuil, 1993–2002).

© Éditions du Seuil, for *Oeuvres complètes, tome I*, 1993 and 2002
© Éditions du Seuil, for *Oeuvres complètes, tome II*, 1993, 1994 and 2002
© Éditions du Seuil, for *Oeuvres complètes, tome III*, 1994 and 2002
© Éditions du Seuil, for *Oeuvres complètes, tome IV*, 1994, 1995 and 2002
© Éditions du Seuil, for *Oeuvres complètes, tome V*, 1995 and 2002

First published in English translation by Seagull Books, 2016
English translation © Chris Turner, 2016

ISBN 978 1 8030 9 276 8

British Library Cataloguing-in-Publication Data
A catalogue record for this book is available from the British Library.

Book designed and typeset by Bishan Samaddar, Seagull Books, Calcutta, India
Printed and bound by WordsWorth India, New Delhi, India

Contents

Pre-Novels

When Claude Bourdet was dismissed as editor of the newspaper *Combat* in 1950, Maurice Nadeau resigned from the editorship of its cultural pages and went on to join Gilles Martinet and Roger Stéphane at the newly founded *France-Observateur*. Nadeau invited Barthes to contribute to the new venture and he responded with a survey on left-wing writing in November 1952 (see Roland Barthes, 'Left-Wing Writers or Left-Wing Literature', *The 'Scandal' of Marxism*. London: Seagull Books, 2015, pp. 27–32), followed by a number of theatre reviews in the early months of 1954. This article, published on 24 June 1954, is a review of three avant-garde novels: Jean Cayrol's *L'Espace d'une nuit* (Seuil; *All in a Night*. London: Faber, 1957), Alain Robbe-Grillet's *Les Gommes* (Ed. de Minuit; *The Erasers*. New York: Grove Press, 1964) and Jean Duvignaud's *Le Piège* (Gallimard). Robbe-Grillet's novel came to be regarded as one of the major founding texts of the French Nouveau Roman while the work of the more reclusive Cayrol is often ascribed to the same loose movement.

Oeuvres complètes, Volume 1, pp. 500–02

Every time someone ventures the idea that there is a crisis of the novel, a critic with the good health of our Literature at heart can be found to reply that the novel *has never been in such fine fettle*, since an enormous number of them are being published. But this is to conceive the crisis in excessively quantitative terms; it is a phenomenon that in no way precludes proliferation. One need only recall the state of our poetry in the eighteenth century, or of our romantic theatre—crisis amid abundance. From a distance, those particular crises are clear for all to see.

Only they are crises of structure, not of production. This is, perhaps, what is happening today with the novel, if you will concede that most of the creditable and original works currently being published are problematical novels in which the fiction is accompanied by a questioning of the basic categories of novelistic creation, as though, since the ideal novel—the innocent novel—is now impossible, literature had principally to say how it is running from itself and killing itself—in short, how it is rejecting itself.

In France this began with Proust. Throughout his enormous *oeuvre*, Proust is always about to write. He has the traditional literary act in his sights, but he constantly puts it off and it is at the end of this period of expectation, an expectation he *never meets*, that the work has been constructed in spite of itself. It was the waiting itself that formed the substance of a work whose *suspended* nature was enough to set the writer speaking.

The most conscious forms of novel-writing today are all part of this Proustian movement by which the writer sets his novel going before our eyes and then consigns it to silence at a point when, a hundred years earlier, he would have barely begun to speak. This seems to me to be the meaning of the work of Jean Cayrol, for example, which is always an open instigation of Literature. In the traditional novel, the novelist seems to be going back within a fiction that is already constituted; he is exploring a depth that is ideally given; he is excavating times, hearts and social relations, each of which is already a very old story. Cayrol, by contrast, doesn't see the novelist's movement as a going back in time but as a slow drift along the surface of a human domain that is yet to be constructed, the structure of which might be said to be constituted at the very point when the book ends. The novelist's function is no longer endoscopic in this case, but consists in getting alongside a world that is familiar but unusual, because it is one that has yet to be born, a world for which the classical novel, the ready-armed novel, would be a deadly and unbearable form of expression.

Robbe-Grillet's project (there is nothing exhaustive about these examples; I take them randomly from recent reading) isn't, like Cayrol's, to cast into doubt the novelist's *familiarity* with his world; it attacks another prejudice of the classical novel, one that is just as entrenched as the subjectivity of the creative artist— the organization of literary space. We should note that, of all the dimensions of the novel, Time was the first to suffer the novelist's attempts at its destruction or restructuring, and the reader is familiar these days with the flashback technique or the use of simultaneity. Space, for its part, is still more or less intact.

Robbe-Grillet is attempting to introduce a new mix of space and time into narrative—what might be called an Einsteinian dimension of objects. This is particularly important since we are still living, in literary terms, with a purely Newtonian view of the universe: Albert Camus or André Breton describe a landscape the way Chateaubriand or Lamartine did. Painting solved this problem of the simultaneous figuration of planes in motion long ago. Literature hasn't yet done so. The theatre has partially solved it, as can be seen in some passages in Eugène Ionesco's *How to Get Rid of It*.[1] Does it really trouble or surprise anyone to have

---

1 The reference is to Eugène Ionesco's 'absurdist' play, *Amédée, ou comment s'en débarrasser* (*Amédée or How to Get Rid of It*, 1954). The 'it' in question is a slowly expanding corpse. Barthes refers to the play here by what is now regarded as its subtitle. [Trans.]

ROLAND BARTHES

the stage split and to see the action, which the actors are apparently watching in front of them, actually going on behind?

Another attempt at breaking up the novel is seen in the work of Jean Duvignaud, where the novel shuns its own form and turns into theatre or, to put it another way, develops an extraordinary reversibility between fiction and reality, an ambiguous bracketing-together of the real view and the view in the mirror. This mirroring is something like the theme of the age; *Hamlet* and its play within a play might be said to provide the archetype. For Duvignaud, narrative is no longer the all-powerful word of the novelist but a dual thing: the narrator both looks and is looked at, and the creator is constantly menaced by his creations, while all these are threatened by the potential irruption of their own images. The novel leaves its display case and becomes an aggression against—a devouring of—its consumer.

These works are the products of very different minds. What they have in common, which is no doubt a feature of the age, is a single way of focusing the gaze. We might say that the novel, after centuries of deep vision, has finally set itself the task of exploring surfaces. Insofar as it is total, this is a new course of action—the aim is no longer to describe everyday life with the exploratory meticulousness of the *verismo* novelist but to probe into the very heart of description and to cast fundamental doubt on the commonest, most accepted elements of novelistic technique: space, objects and the distances that may separate the novelist from the world and his creation.

There is scarcely any need to state, then, that psychology, psychoanalysis, metaphysics or affectivity are absent from these works, since it is their essential aim to bring human beings back from the depths of their domain to the surface. Certain of these attempts still have something undeniably experimental about them. But that doesn't mean at all that we face the danger of an inhuman literature being ushered in. Quite the contrary—this calling into question of the simplest elements of the traditional novel will be justified if it leads to ridding fiction of the age-old lies of 'depth'. What wonderful pathos a literature concerned purely with earthly matters should afford us.

Recovering Unburied Treasure

The next four essays were all written for the *Bulletin de la Guilde du Livre* in February 1955. This publication began life as the internal newsletter of a Swiss book club founded at Lausanne by Albert Mermoud in 1936, but in the post-war years it acquired a prominent place as one of the few serious French-language literary reviews on the Swiss scene, having only one notable competitor in the form of *La Gazette littéraire*, the weekly literary supplement of *La Gazette de Lausanne*. The Guilde du livre, which was also well known for hosting an annual literary prize that rewarded its beneficiary with the sizeable sum of 5,000 francs, ceased operations in 1977.

The poet and novelist Claude Roy is the author of a celebrated series of autobiographical works spanning several decades of the twentieth century. His *Trésor de la poésie populaire française*, which is reviewed here, was published by the Guilde du livre of Lausanne and also by the Paris-based publisher of poetry Éditions Seghers in their series 'Poésie de tous les temps' in 1954. Claire Vervin is credited alongside Roy for her part in helping to select the texts. The book was reissued by Plon in June 1999.

Oeuvres complètes, Volume 1, p. 569–74

It is a common prejudice today to believe that France has no folklore—or very little. Patriarchal times seem so long ago for us as French people and it is such a long time since the Revolution ingrained the norms of bourgeois thought into our critical habits that, as we see it, the idea of popular culture is most often one of extension rather than quality. We are scarcely minded to acknowledge its substantive nature. We believe quite simply that popular art is, in the best of cases, an eternal art disseminated to the masses as one of the generous benefits of republican education. If, by some chance, we become aware of the historical depth of popular activity in the fields of art or poetry, we do so on the back of some sort of Romantic revival: For how many of us is French popular poetry nothing more than those songs of the Valois region rediscovered by Nerval?

And the national conception of poetry that has been handed down to us adds further to this indifference. We have been told so often that French poetry is not lyrical, that the French have no great poets except the so-called *rhétoriqueurs*[1] and that French literary art is distinguished for its discursive forms, whereas other peoples with less prestigious cultures have only ever been able to be poets—and naive poets at that. We have been taught so much to pride ourselves on our thought—even if it means jettisoning the ballast of our images—that we readily accept being a people without poetic annals, popular art or memorial culture.

It is this tissue of wrong-headed—and probably self-interested—clichés that Claude Roy's anthology vigorously, joyfully and, it should be said, triumphantly destroys. His *Trésor de la poésie populaire française* provides an authoritative survey of the field: to have brought all these fine texts together seems to me as important a literary event as the discovery of a precious manuscript. Particularly as, up until now, though laudable for the care and patient labour involved, collections of popular poetry—extremely rare and the work of scholars or regionalists—have always had an unattractive, archival character. They have had a fusty air to them, smacking of curiosity or, at best, affectionate sentiment, but very rarely of life and, even less, of literature.

1 The reference is to a poetry of sophisticated rhyme schemes and metre and complex word play. The grands *rhétoriqueurs* were a group of poets working in Flanders, Northern France and Burgundy in the late fifteenth and early sixteenth centuries. [Trans.]

Yet what shines out in Claude Roy's anthology is precisely the triumph of literature. In his preface, Roy explains very clearly that popular poetry isn't necessarily a collective, anonymous work of unknown origin— in no sense is it a sort of magical emanation from ancestral lands, as was so often argued in Romantic or post-Romantic times. Popular poems often have known authors and it isn't in any way their origins that establish them as popular art but the intention behind them or, more exactly, the use to which history has put them. What marks them out, says Roy perceptively, is *being successful*. It is the people's approval of a work, which is often as inspired as the most precious of literary texts, that makes that work a popular one. Contrary to class poetry, popular poetry is defined first and foremost at the level of consumption, not at the level of the muses. And this is the first lesson in criticism Roy's book provides: against current literary history, which is always a history of privileged moments of inspiration and creation, it is possible to range another history that would draw its material not from the singularity of literature but from its *sociability*.

This clears the way for many a clarification: for example, that we might very well conceive of a great literature free of the age-old taboo of inalterability. The image of the high-culture poem always contains a requirement of changeless formal perfection: the work is just as fiercely owned by the author as the field is by the peasant or the wall by the bourgeois—to change a word or a comma in it is a crime as heinous as moving a tree, hedge or stone or altering the slope of a roof. This appropriation freezes the poem. By preserving it from adulteration, it takes from it much of its nobility, for it isn't possible to *be of use* without experiencing wear and tear, without the molecules and surfaces of the work undergoing change. Popular poetry isn't written poetry, it doesn't recognize changelessness as a sacred value. It accepts that the same poem may change or be added to; it may run out of steam or, conversely, gain new impetus. But the reward for so much freedom is that such poetry follows history—its sociability isn't solely extensive, affecting varied classes of human beings and occupations, it is also intensive, grouping different layers of history within a single work and accompanying humanity in the successive phases of its understanding. It is, in some measure, to cultivated poetry (or at least to the image traditional criticism presents of it) what the barter economy was to the economy based on gold; doubtless gold doesn't wear out, but history rapidly lent something inhuman to that purity. The treasure of higher poetry is a hidden treasure whereas that of popular poetry was always out in the open and exposed, even to adulteration, and it is we who have devalued it by hiding it away. In bringing it out into the open once more, Claude Roy has restored a healthy glow to it—something which comes to it fulsomely from its circulation, as is the case with all living things.

What Claude Roy's book enables us to contrast effectively are, of course, types of use, not poetic essences. In fact, for all the differences between the *fate* of written poetry and that of popular poetry, there are few differences in their natures. What is clear to see from this *Trésor . . .* is the identity of the two forms of poetry (Roy emphasizes this himself). Throughout these poems, which stretch over a period covering the best part of our national history, we can *recognize*—with an intense sense of familiarity—the very archetypes of our great poetic moments, from the Middle Ages to the Surrealists and Éluard (with the exception of the classical writers, who were resolved to have no popular currency). These texts have the essential daring touches of what is by common consent called great literature: pithy turns of phrase, an irrational element, the poise of a language that never gets carried away with its own feats of brilliance and rejects rhetorical self-indulgence—in short, that wonderful state of *ineloquence* we have come, in the past, to recognize as the strength of the great authors. Take one detail, for example: with what restraint these verses are rounded off, shunning the brashness of traditional clausulae.

We should like to imagine a philosophy of literary history that would, after a survey of known poets, present this spread of popular poems as a Platonic archetype of poetry, for it is definitely an idea of literature we have here, an idea of which our *belles-lettres* are, in a sense, a historical reflection. Reading at random among the popular proverbs that close this *Trésor*— 'God tempers the wind to the shorn lamb' or 'The key one uses always shines bright'—am I not reaching within myself to a state of immediate self-evidence, to senses of nourishment and delight that underlie all literature as a thing of happiness and release?

And, at the same time, what is established is clearly the idea of a good literature. Another virtue of Claude Roy's anthology would be to enable us, then, to develop a morality of literature. This *Trésor de la poésie populaire* renders sham poetry even more intolerable and makes it easier to demystify the high priests of academic poetry, the Barbediennes[2] of confected literature. Compare the popular songs of war with jingoistic couplets, the real work-songs of human beings with the hymns to labour penned by well-intentioned poets in their studies; truth and poetry are on the same side here. It is the same with the great Romantic themes: Nature, Death and Love are hymned from a *human* standpoint, not in their conceptual relations.

If I had to teach French children, I would very willingly lay aside dictations from the writings of

---

2 Ferdinand Barbedienne was a metalworker and manufacturer who, among other things, provided small-scale reproductions of artistic bronzes to an emergent mass market from the late 1830s onwards. The firm which he founded with Achille Colas ceased operations in 1954. [Trans.]

André Theuriet and recitations of the works of Jean Aicard and, in spite of its misplaced (though marvellously euphonious) elisions, grammatical errors and incorrect 'liaisons' (though these too are charming), look to Claude Roy's *Trésor* for my class' educational nourishment. That would be the best way to help the pupils to move imperceptibly to a delight in more consciously crafted literary works later. No sort of gulf exists between a popular love poem such as 'Amour, tu n'entends point' and verses by Apollinaire, and our right-thinking critics would be less surprised by the irrationality of modern poetic language if Claude Roy's fine book had formed the basis of their literary studies.

The Man-Eater

This second piece for *Le Bulletin de la Guilde du livre* is an essay on Zola's novel *Nana*. The novel, one of the acknowledged masterworks of French Naturalism, was first published in 1880 by Éditions Fasquelle as the ninth instalment of Zola's Rougon-Macquart series.

Barthes's essay coincides with the Guilde du livre's reissuing of the book in a numbered edition with an imitation-leather binding in June 1955. That same year, the Club français du livre also issued a new edition with illustrations by Georges Bellenger and a preface by Armand Lanoux. The Guilde du livre's version was prefaced by the one-time Dadaist Georges Ribemont-Dessaignes.

Oeuvres complètes, Volume 1, pp. 587–90

Nana is the daughter of Coupeau, the alcoholic worker in Zola's *L'Assommoir*.[1] A bad actress and a good courtesan, a whole society of men is gathered around her—bankers, journalists, officers, aristocrats and senior civil servants of Napoleon III's regime. She lives off that society and does so royally, destroying fortunes, driving some to their ruin, others to theft and yet others to suicide. When she has destroyed everything around her, Nana departs, being spirited away for a time to a mythical Russia. Then she returns to die of smallpox in Paris on the very day war is declared in 1870.

The symbolic arc of the work is clear: Nana, the child of the people, corrupts the bourgeoisie; she sends them to their doom and herself with them. Corresponding to the military debacle of 1871 is a thoroughgoing

---

1 Translated into English by Robin Buss as *The Drinking Den* (London: Penguin, 2003). [Trans.]

disintegration of imperial France; this goes much deeper and is both physical and moral. The entire society of the Second Empire, corrupted by Nana, collapses—the people has its revenge. However, alienated by the bourgeoisie, it is itself dragged into the fall it has caused—the whole of France succumbs under the impact of imperial fascism.

Nana is truly an epic book—not only by the marvellous excess of its depictions but also by its very tempo, which is the familiar tempo of catastrophe. Zola wishes to paint a process of deterioration, a debacle, and the entire movement of his story is subordinated to that intention. For example, the initial tempo of the book is slow, meticulous, indolent. We are in that happy state where the scope of pleasures expands and the author lingers long over a single evening. Then, as the rot sets in and men become increasingly entangled in Nana's toils, the narrative speeds up and months at the end pass like minutes at the beginning. The disintegration process moves at a gathering pace which stunningly conveys its relentlessness.

Another epic feature: Nana is herself the victim of the havoc she causes, without gaining anything by it and, we might even say, without learning anything from it. We know that the movement of decline, of progressive downfall is the very movement of tragedy (as with Oedipus, for example, led into solitude and exile by the progressive discovery of his identity; and the Shakespearian kings, dethroned by some solar successor, so many individuals gradually banished into outer darkness). Why, then, is *Nana* an epic work and not a tragic one? Because tragic heroes advance on two fronts: as they plunge deeper into misfortune, they gain a more intense awareness of their humanity; they discover their own worth and the very excess of their suffering in the end affords them wisdom and it is precisely this that represents their triumph over destiny (Oedipus is happy at Colonus, Richard II becomes himself in prison). There is nothing of the sort with Nana—she has no tragic power because she has no power of awareness. To the end she remains a mere instrument, a detonating or corroding mechanism (depending on the episode), set down unmercifully in Second Empire society and carrying out her mission of destruction with no chance whatever of redemption. And so *Nana* is truly an epic, the narrative of a movement, the awareness of which is at no point situated within the work itself, and in which there is never that kind of soul-searching on the part of characters that we find in tragedy. Zola remains the only consciousness of this catastrophe, because it was his intention that it should have no other consciousness than the historical; he is the—human, yet fearsome—bard who depicts this dreadful panorama of a society going under but keeps it some way out in front of us so that we can see it better and avoid entanglement in its collapse.

This epic character of *Nana* must also be attributed to a technique commonly employed by Zola (technique isn't quite the right word, since it is in reality the very principle of his art), which consists in reducing the world to a small number of sensations that become something like its sensory essences (this is what, in the classical epic, was referred to as the use of epithets—such as 'grey-eyed Athena'). Zola's depiction is always obsessive: for example, love is only ever presented as generating warmth, and Zola never alludes to desire without immediately attaching this same thematics to it—the thematics of heat. This is an admirable technique of useful distortion and offers confirmation once again that genius is, first and foremost, obstinacy.

This means that Zola arrives at truth by other paths than naturalism (despite academic classifications). Zola is an epic writer, a writer who distorts— he distorts in the direction of an exemplary, not a natural, truth. He doesn't copy reality but expresses it—expressing in the sense of *squeezing out*, as one might squeeze juice from a fruit. In other words, far from reconstituting a thousand details and nuances by rendering the exact dosage of the original, he searches out and selects the essential theme and turns it into a kind of key point hammered home throughout the book. What Zola renders in this way are types, but tangible types, endowed not so much with the algebraic psychology of the classical moralists as with flesh, blood and humours in which we can read their condition, their weakness, their vulgarity or their failings. There is, moreover, nothing gratuitous about this fleshly thematics—it is intended to represent evidence of insight, to contribute to a reading of history that goes deeper than the pleasures of novel-reading.

This brilliant distortion enabled Zola to depict Second Empire society in *Nana* with the kind of tremendous distance achieved by an ethnologist studying a Kwakiutl tribe. I have just pointed out that, with Zola, we are looking not at a scientific but a distorting objectivity which consists in taking the targeted swathe of humanity as a real object that one never speaks about without attaching the same two or three adjectives to it. Now, Zola's power of objectivization (not objectivity) is enormous, particularly when it applies to these men and women of the Second Empire. To our great stupefaction, we find ourselves faced with an anthropology that seems as outlandish to us as that of Papua. We even have the impression that these human beings, some of whom could quite simply have been our grandparents (though that would be rather unflattering), had a different morphology from our own, that they had other temperaments, feelings, gestures, odours and appetites, generally living in physiques different from our own. And this to such a degree that we find it difficult, at times, to understand the ravages wrought on all sides by Nana—it seems almost as improbable to us, in emotional terms, as the seductive power of the Hottentot Venus. (Yet this is of little importance: *Nana* remains a thrilling book since its beauty and its force of persuasion lie in the materiality of what it demonstrates, not the verisimilitude of what it suggests).

This does not mean that Zola's distorting genius is alone responsible for this unfamiliarity. In reality— and this is a fact worthy of attention—we are usually much more familiar with earlier periods of our past. Our adventure novels, our historical theatre (how many plays there are about Magellan, Columbus, Savonarola, Louis XIV, etc.), our cinema and all our imaginative arts find it much easier to deal with classical or pre-classical man—the Spanish grandee, the musketeer or the marquis—than the frock-coated individual of the Second Empire. It is an age that has fallen out of favour with us; it doesn't even have the caricatural charm of 1900. For us, it is a period without credibility or attraction; it is a bizarre time—both vulgar and baroque. In terms of human history, however, it was deep down a thrilling, though politically bleak age; and the swathe of commercial ventures associated with it, not to mention the fantastic development of modern types of business, ought to excite our curiosity far more than a royal procession or a Romantic interior.

Nana will not reduce the degree of remoteness we feel from the mentalities of those days. Far from it. Yet by lending an excess of colour to that world, Zola forces us here and now to view the spectacle with a historical eye. Far from boring us, as so many novelists have done, by describing a barely historicized instance of the eternal Woman as eternal man-eater, Zola sets this alleged universal before us in its historical particularity. And we cease to sigh and begin to judge. We understand better then the aim of this epic art—by putting the human back into history, the artist invites us to form an active awareness of it. Nana, the *femme fatale*, ceases to be a timeless character and acquires an individuality whose very strangeness evokes judgement rather than identification. It is for this reason that, despite the fearsomely caustic nature of its depictions, *Nana* is a very fine book, a very great book and I would say, if the word did not bear some hereditary taint of tedium belied by the powerful arguments that recommend it here, a book of civic responsibility.

Maupassant and the Physics of Misfortune

This third piece for *Le Bulletin de la Guilde du livre*, written in January 1956, focuses on the writings of Guy de Maupassant, particularly the short stories for which he is rightly celebrated. Maupassant, whose literary activity was at its height in the 1880s, descended into madness after a failed suicide attempt in January 1892. His early death at the age of 43 was probably precipitated by syphilis which he is thought to have contracted as a young man, though Barthes does not refer to that directly.

Oeuvres complètes, Volume 1, pp. 640–3

How the short story differs from the novel is a question that has often been asked. I believe, myself, that what is at issue is a certain use of catastrophe. The real, true novel, the novel that takes you over slowly and surely, is most often simply the story of a decline: novelistic misfortune is never pure, it has a density to it that is more existential than conceptual. With the short story, precisely the opposite applies: misfortune exists in the short story as a solitary, incontrovertible fact (ill fortune or good—it's all the same). Situations do not follow one another or fade; they clash and precipitate collapse. There is something organic about catastrophe in the novel, something mechanical about it in the short story. This is probably why the short story can easily be a vehicle for a kind of didacticism—something definitely happens and it is something conclusive (whereas a genuine novel, such as *War and Peace*, remains profoundly ambiguous). The short story is a creation that is often more intellective than oneiric; the novel is more or less always a *passion story* of misfortune while the short story is more its *demonstration*. And it is perhaps insofar as the French have generally preferred the literature of moral evaluation to that of emotional investment that they have managed to write excellent short stories.

Maupassant's short stories also take it as their mission to demonstrate a catastrophe. Beneath their prim and proper disguise as anthology-pieces-for-young-foreign-language-learners, they are fearsome stories in which the calamity is always so pure that, were it not for a certain *vulgarity* that was a feature of the age, it could pass for the modern form of the tragic. This is because there are in these stories of Maupassant the two great age-old figures of defeat: Fear and Powerlessness.

We know that the first of these themes originates in—or is, at least, underpinned by—the very illness from which Maupassant suffered: he died a madman after years of mental disturbance involving depression, hallucinations and anxieties. Horror stories abound in Maupassant's work, and fear immediately assumes a pathological aspect in his writings—it is an irrational feeling, a sense of panic, a kind of all-consuming intoxication arising not out of the sense of impending misfortune but from the uncertainty and mystery aroused by the approach of some formless, indefinable catastrophe. There is here quite an exact transposition of pathological anxiety, in which the sufferer feels his body falling prey to an external force that holds it in its grip, without his being able to *put a name* to that force. Maupassant's fear isn't in any way the product of a metaphysical process of guilt—it is a primitive, elemental state and hence totally objective.

For this reason, external surroundings play a preponderant role in these stories. The fear is essentially sustained by objects (not by persons) and those objects are invested with a terrifying degree of supernatural power. They include bells (ship's bells and bells rung for the dead), snow, monstrous dogs and mysterious drums (as in certain cowboy films). Such accoutrements are rather crude and childish; they are not as 'classy' as those deployed by Edgar Allen Poe. But this doesn't mean that Maupassant's language of panic fear is inauthentic. We know that when certain psychopaths set about writing poetry, they don't necessarily produce work like Antonin Artaud's; more often they write the conventional verse of a François Coppée. Maupassant's terrors are rhetorical too, but that doesn't mean they were not experienced. Moreover, it is probable that Naturalism, which initially presented itself as a form of anti-Romantic self-restraint, played a part in toning down the more excessive expressions of strangeness. This was an age that often strove after the baroque (for example, the Goncourt brothers, Huysmans), but never achieved it, at least to our modern eyes, except in Barbedienne bronzes[1] and Henri II

1 See p. 13 [Trans.]

dining rooms. The epidemic of vulgarity that raged at the time affected even the greatest geniuses and was only really dispelled with the arrival of Proust.

But that same vulgarity, unhelpful to Maupassant when it makes the terror element in his short stories a little too familiar, aids him admirably when it comes to describing the social class from which it is generally recognized to have sprung—the petty bourgeoisie. Because of the misunderstanding generated by anthologies, ever avid for local colour, it is his rural stories set in Normandy that are the best known whereas the urban petty bourgeoisie was the primary—we might even say obsessive—object of Maupassant's art. It was probably an important discovery of Naturalism to have seen that the French petty bourgeoisie, elevated to a particular political role in 1848, constituted a historic totality and a national entity, defined by an economy, an aesthetic and a morality, and hence appropriate for depiction with as much 'local' colour as Balzac's aristocracy or George Sand's peasants. Once again, Flaubert is the great initiator here and Maupassant is in every respect much more the disciple of Flaubert than he is of Zola, to whom the artificial identity of literary movements attaches him.

Flaubert and Maupassant both tried to define the petty-bourgeois ethic (in part, probably, because they suffered daily from it), but took different paths to do so. In some pages of his novels, in the extraordinary *Bouvard and Pécuchet* and in his *Dictionary of Received*

Ideas, Flaubert was particularly intent upon deriding the petty bourgeoisie: he reproduced—that is to say, distantiated and criticized—the static alienation of its language. The very form of the short story involved Maupassant in a less subtle yet at the same time more dynamic description—it is not so much the petty bourgeoisie's stupidity as its powerlessness that was described there; hence, a certain silent pathos that underlies all Maupassant's stories and has about it something of that sense of catastrophe I mentioned at the beginning. Maupassant's description represents an extremely accurate historical analysis—in the great capitalist boom of the latter half of the nineteenth century, the state-employed petty bourgeois, missing out on both the expansive development of business and the awakening of labour-movement consciousness, experienced an inevitable sense of powerlessness. Being more or less parasitic on the state at a point when the bureaucracy was by no means strong, they were doomed—barring fantasy solutions (such as the return of a rich 'American uncle', as in Maupassant's short story 'Uncle Jules')—to hopeless poverty. The block on their social mobility was all the more painful to this class of people as they were constantly in contact with the prestige of money and witnessed the material comfort of *arrivistes* at first hand, though, alas, these things remained a mere mirage for them (though penniless, Mme Loisel *can* go to the minister's ball).

Maupassant grasped this fragile, subtle state remarkably well, in which a social class is both alienated and dreamy-eyed, fascinated by the possibility of rising in society yet ignorant of the real obstacles that prevent it from doing so. Hence all his 'social' tales (there are far more of them than people think) are situated on the borderline between dreaming and waking. The catastrophe I spoke of a moment ago always consists in an insuperably stark social reverse— it is alienation in all its hideousness and, also, with all its pathos. The characters, like people 'possessed', appear to have the seeds of tragic catastrophe within them—blindness, excess, a mad desire to seem 'more than they are'. Almost all Maupassant's short stories are dramas of social vanity.

These stories most often have a ternary structure that very well expresses the catastrophic, chaotic character of this world. In an initial phase, petty-bourgeois alienation is shown as it really is: a shabby life, involving a poverty that is all the more acute for having at all costs to retain a mask of decency, with sordid details— dirty tablecloths, 'maids' on the cheap, a 'careful' lifestyle, etc. Then, in a second phase, alienation falls prey to dreaming. The characters are carried away by a sudden rush of social vanity that causes them to overstep, if only for a day, the limits of their social condition. Mme Loisel, the wife of a minor civil servant, borrows an expensive diamond necklace in order to 'be someone' at the minister's ball; a clerk in a government department gives in to the urge to extend assistance to an ecclesiastic who flatters him; an aristocrat fallen on hard times hires a coach and horses to make a show on the Champs-Élysées. And in a third phase comes the catastrophe: Mme Loisel loses her diamond necklace and will spend her whole life paying for it; the ecclesiastic turns out to be a crook; the coach and horses knocks over an old woman who will have to be kept for the rest of her days. In the end, all the characters find themselves a little more mired in poverty and servitude, alienated more deeply by their insane attempts at social climbing—everything collapses into ridicule or greater destitution.

Minor as they may be, these catastrophes are total, pure, stark and irretrievable. There is a fearful historical pessimism in all this. But that pessimism isn't illusory, because Maupassant has caught the state-employed petty bourgeoisie in what is actually a hopeless phase of its development. That sense of misfortune was probably in tune with a certain physical inclination towards catastrophe that was particular to Maupassant and that is attested elsewhere by all his tales of hallucination. And it is perhaps this pathos, facile despite being genuinely experienced, that has to some extent thrown critics off the scent of his real power—Maupassant is one of the great writers of our literature who managed to describe in depth a social alienation which he demystified with great nobility.

The Cathedral
of Novels

The fourth and final article for *Le Bulletin de la Guilde du livre*, written in March 1957, is a review of Victor Hugo's *Notre-Dame de Paris*, a work first translated into English by Frederic Schoberl in 1833 as *The Hunchback of Notre-Dame*. That has subsequently been the name given to no fewer than six film adaptations of the story (not to mention two musicals and a ballet), though Hugo's original title has generally been restored in other, later translations of the novel—for example, *Notre Dame of Paris* (John Sturrock trans.) (London: Penguin, 1978).

Oeuvres complètes, Volume 1, pp. 873–6

As a novel, *Notre-Dame of Paris* is very much like the historic building that is its main character: it has the same motley mix of parts, some of them outmoded, others still vividly beautiful; the same unevenness of wear and tear and, most importantly, the same wonderful ultimate unity, despite the diversity of its detail. And just as the best tourist—by which I mean the wisest and the best rewarded—is the one who is able to accept a building in its entirety, so the best reader of Hugo is the one who isn't too concerned with untangling in this book the vulgar from the genuinely touching, the puerile from the sophisticated, the archaic from the avant-garde. Both as cathedral and as novel, you have to take *Notre-Dame of Paris* as something all of a piece, for better or for worse. It's a gamble worth risking: shut yourself away one Sunday with *Notre-Dame of Paris* and, once you are over the irritating excess of leaden humour, the annoying Latin quotations in sham medieval taste and some boring, philosophically unsubtle disquisitions, the spell is worked, that prodigious fascination great writing produces takes over and image is transmuted into reality.

For *Notre-Dame of Paris* is in every sense the book of closeting and confinement, which is why it is a voluptuous read. When they say that, in Hugo's work, the old cathedral forms a world, this is, I think, not so much a reference to its vastness as to its closed nature. Frollo and Quasimodo reign over a finite, complete, hermetic place (the last adjective is happily ambiguous) that is entirely sufficient unto itself, materially and spiritually. In that place, the age-old marvel of every autarkic universe comes to pass, the preternatural state of independence and warmth that is the ultimate object of all the great forms of imagination—the child's, the poetic and the neurotic.

A place of shelter is only fully experienced in its happy essence if it is confronted with the open space against which it defines itself: the ship is pitted against the sea, the castle against the plain, the cabin against the forest. Notre-Dame stands over against Paris, but the stroke of genius is to have conceived the confrontation of the historic building and its surroundings not as a juxtaposition of two spaces but as a dialogue between a towering height and a horizontal expanse. By contrast with our ordinary dreams of refuge, Notre-Dame doesn't lie deep in the ground but is a tall edifice. Or it is, at least, if we may put it this way, deep by virtue of height—it is at its summit that one is most shut away. For Hugo, there is no *outside*, only a *below*. And it is the marvellous picture of Paris seen from a bird's-eye view, a topological panorama that adds physical clarity, so to speak, to intellective clarity (these pages are a model of intelligent geography), for the height of the vantage point provides the reader with that impression of preternatural ease and limitless power which air travel was to achieve a century later and which Bachelard has analysed so well, with regard to poetry, in his book on air and dreams.[1] Another great Romantic, Michelet, had also derived thoroughly modern effects from these overarching views, which turn the reader into a veritable god, comprehending historical and terrestrial space (though isn't all space historical?) in proportion as he *creates* it with his eyes.

By its towering heights, then, the cathedral has power in a bodily sense over the surrounding space— it *comprehends* that space in both senses of the word, and the reader does so with it. But this is a function— we might term it a poetic function—that manifests itself only when it is, so to speak, Hugo inhabiting Notre-Dame. For the characters in the novel, the cathedral remains essentially a closed space—it is, above all, a place of asylum. Admittedly, that place of asylum has, first, a powerful anecdotal role: from Clopin Trouillefou to Louis XI, all the characters ultimately

---

1 Gaston Bachelard, *L'Air et les songes: essai sur l'imagination du mouvement* (Paris: José Corti, 1943). [Trans.]

find themselves interconnected around the abduction of Esmeralda in the cathedral. But the place of asylum also—and most importantly—has a poetic role; Notre-Dame as refuge affords all the joy of a world completed, a world as full as can be, the internal life of which, sufficient unto itself, suspends and denies everything around it—time, space, hatred, political developments out in the wider world. Notre-Dame has everything—even flowers, growing out of its stones! The place of asylum is all the happier here for the fact that Hugo has, once again, managed to define it by its height, substituting for the age-old dream of a cave or terrestrial lair—in short, for *depth*—the image of the terrace in the skies, the hanging garden. A little later, another great novelist, Jules Verne (a popular writer if ever there was one), stoked the daydreams of so many children and adults by similarly combining depth and height in the refuge of Cyrus Smith and his companions in his novel *The Mysterious Island*.[2]

Moreover, the mythic character of this closed cathedral is fully revealed in the episode of its defence. Quasimodo keeps the building closed against the entire world and it is, in fact, the place itself, endowed with a kind of organic force, which defends itself while the monstrous but tender-hearted hunchback—acting as a kind of magical mediator—merely *presents* the

2 Jules Verne, *L'Île mystérieuse* (Paris: Hetzel, 1875). [Trans.]

defence of an immense body that protects itself by abandoning chunks of its mineral flesh. The assault of the *Truands*, who are crawling, earthbound men armed with a weaponry that also belongs to the element of earth (rams, beams, wooden ladders) is countered by an attack from supernatural substances—molten lead, which is both liquid and fire, and air in the form of the void into which Quasimodo pitches the assailants, and into which he will at the last hurl Frollo, a traitor to the jealous closure of the building.

The plot itself, that counterpointing of events and the operation of fate (remarkably well handled by Hugo, by the way), can only really be understood in relation to this closed status that defines the cathedral—everything happens here because people want to leave or enter, to claim or violate asylum, to abuse or submit to it. Outside, far from the deep sense of the place, lies the restless, grotesque, inessential, secular world: the king, the officers of the law, the thieves (though the *cour des miracles* picks up, in weakened form, on the theme of confinement). Between that open world and the closed church is a torn and divi-ded token, a riven object whose fateful movement, powerless to find a resting place, is the undoing of everyone—Esmeralda. And in the building itself, good and evil—Quasimodo, the genius of closure incarnate, imprisoned irretrievably in the stones, in his ugliness, deafness and impossible love. And Frollo, punished horribly for having shat-tered the—mineral and spiritual—matrix within which he had begun to be happy.

Thus, beneath the distraction of 'local colour', beneath the plot, beneath the avowed philosophy of history, Hugo has hatched a true cosmic drama, a clash of substances, those ideal old substances which, diversely modulated, have fuelled folk tales and works of literature for centuries. It isn't its earthiness that makes *Notre-Dame of Paris* a great popular work (though the book is a bulky one and doesn't partake of the virtues of the legendary French novel of the *Princesse de Clèves* or Stendhalian type), but what we have to call, despite the hackneyed nature of the term, its *poetry*: namely, that power to accomplish, in the reader's innermost soul—in that obscure part of the psyche where the physical and the mental mix—the very movement by which the human being accepts or rejects, transforms and assimilates the great states of matter: emptiness and fullness, depth and height, the open and the closed—the deep life of the body that accompanies with its dream the whole of human history.

Round Table
Discussions

Oeuvres complètes, Volume 1, pp. 960–2

This text appeared in the 'Mythologies' column in *Les Lettres nouvelles*, though it did so after the book *Mythologies* had been published (1957)—on 25 March 1959.

'Nouveau Roman' (literally, New Novel) is a label that was originally applied by journalists to a group of novelists who were each working with new, experimental forms of literary narration—and were largely published by Jérôme Lindon's Éditions de Minuit or, to a lesser degree, Éditions Gallimard. While there is much argument about precisely who was a 'new novelist', Barthes identifies a core group here who more or less accepted the designation and appeared at events under its banner. The writers he refers to initially are Alain Robbe-Grillet, whose *Pour un nouveau roman* became a sort of retrospective manifesto for the movement, Nathalie Sarraute, Michel Butor and Claude Simon. Robert Pinget, who was also a 'member' of this loose grouping, is mentioned further on in the article.

While Barthes was critical of the 'media circus' surrounding the Nouveau Roman, he was generally sympathetic to its literary aims. See 'A Personal Statement on Robbe-Grillet', p. 51.

Yet another Round Table discussion—and on the Nouveau Roman again (this time in *Les Lettres françaises*). How many times is this collective entity called Sarraute-Robbe-Grillet-Butor-Simon going to expatiate around a microphone? And what truth are they trying to convey? Does each of them see more clearly into the others?—or into themselves? Can each of them persuade their opponents of even an atom of their truth? No, this is just a formulaic gathering and the participants are probably under no illusions and merely 'playing the game', because a writer today believes he has to be present everywhere he is called on to be. And they are there perhaps, also, merely out of frailty, like that ancient people which, according to Michelet, perished because they couldn't say no.

Yet this formula isn't an innocent one. First of all, the dialogue it sets up is not only illusory but also contrary to the very basis of Literature; we might say that Literature, at least in our present society, begins at the point where dialogue falls silent. It is historically inevitable in the bourgeois world that the writer is defined by the radical character of his words, which are simultaneously tyranny and heartbreak, an oppressive and an unhappy consciousness. Writing is precisely that contradiction which turns a failure of communication into a secondary communication, words directed to others but without the other being present. Not only can dialogue between writers do nothing to overcome this powerlessness but it duplicates and mystifies it. The two terrors are intimately related—they can only be concealed by harmful or derisory techniques: by emptying out ideas (there is never anything in these Round Table discussions) and multiplying formulaic concessions, a weak way of exorcizing an act that is, by definition, lethal ('to a degree, I share your opinion', 'I agree, but . . .', 'So-and-so is quite right, however . . .'). Merely to offer a work of literature to the world is such a weighty matter that the writer cannot feel an authentic need to uphold or defend it. For the writer, dialogue can only be tactical—it cannot relate to the very nature of a literary work. He may forget the work, but he can never *adapt it to a purpose*. Having been a terrorist while writing his work, he becomes thoroughly liberal when he delivers it. Being both radical and indifferent, he is doubly a stranger to dialogue: aggressively while he is creating, and passively once that creation becomes, for him, a thing of the past.

As a social institution, the Round Table discussion clearly tends to soften this conflict. The operation consists in re-establishing the artificial continuity of the personality, in making creation dependent upon a faith, hence making it answerable; and upon a profession, hence naturalizing the limits of writing which are, in fact, implacable. The assumption is that the writer could express himself in any of several different languages, as though one might attribute to words on the same subject at one point an expressive and, at another, a communicative function, depending on what effect is being sought. This is the myth of the Round Table—that the very matter of solitude can magically become subject to liberal agreement; that creation can become *purposeful comment*. 'A row between Pingaud and Robbe-Grillet? No, they're simply coming to an understanding' we read in the caption to a photo in which we see the two writers bent over their contributions to the debate. That is a good definition of the dialogue between writers: the creation of an understanding between two solitudes, promptly expedited by one of those precious *conjunctions* that are an elegant way of being rid of the other so as to return to the subject of oneself ('indeed', 'agreed', 'however'...).

Not only is the dialogue pointless—when written out, it debases writing. For a writer to speak (on the radio, for example) has at least some value—you can always learn something from his breathing, the substance of his voice. But when that speech is then converted into writing, as though the order and nature of forms of language didn't matter, and when that writing, by a further illusion, is subjected to *serious* correction (as *Lettres françaises* tells us), then this is truly to produce a bastardized, meaningless writing which neither has the clear-cut distance of a written text nor the—at times, poetic—pressure of speech. In short, every Round Table discussion draws from the best of writers the worst of their words—discourse. Now, speech and writing can neither be interchanged nor yoked together, since what there is between them is quite simply of the order of a challenge—writing is made out of a rejection of all other forms of language. The *transcribed* comment plays hypocritically with that rejection—as incoherent as it seems (are these debates not the dross inevitably left over from the occupation of writing?), it implies a natural philosophy of Literature, as though writers had truth dwelling within them and they could simply choose the particular day's way of expressing it: in novelistic form, spoken comments or written discourse, as and when, much as a pretty woman chooses which suit to wear in the morning, as weather, mood and circumstances dictate. In this way the ethical structure of artistic creation is inverted—it is assumed that there is *one* content and *multiple* forms that are more or less costly (the transcribed comment would be the bargain basement item here), whereas Literature is fundamentally an inversion of language, since its form is singular but its meanings innumerable. To write is literally *paradoxical*—it is always to come at the truth obliquely. To record the spoken word and then to write it down is to cheat with the writer's very being; it is to bypass the silence that occupies his centre, the way a fruit has a stone at its centre.

That the Nouveau Roman should reflect on itself, that it should even define itself against its opponents by that reflection, is a necessary triumph over the general obscurantism that is always out to present the writer as an inspired being, that is to say, a stupid one. But this secondary musing is only convincing if it develops in the same vein of seriousness and the same mode as the work on which it seeks to comment—reflection on writing can only be a written thing. At a pinch, a writer can speak of his memories, his plans—in short, of his contingency, without debasing himself in any way; he can speak of his words as a writer only in a language as dense as those words. The only *explanations* from writers that are truly affecting are, generally, voices from beyond the grave—Kafka's *Diaries* or Cesare Pavese's *Diario* [published in English as *The Burning Brand*, 1961]. The self-indulgence of the Nouveau Roman writers as they engage, frivolously and pushily, in pointless and inauthentic dialogues with one another is at odds with the radical character of their literary ethic and the quality of their actual works.

New Pathways of Literary Criticism in France

Oeuvres complètes, Volume 1, pp. 977–80

The following article, a conspectus of recent trends in French literary criticism, was published in May 1959 in the venerable old Yugoslavian newspaper *Politika*. Founded in 1904, *Politika* had generally maintained a strong literary tradition, opening its columns to such prominent authors as Ivo Andrić and Branislav Nušić.

Barthes wrestles particularly with the problem of how to combine a historical dimension, exemplified here by the Romanian-born sociologist of literature Lucien Goldmann, with some promising recent developments in a more psychological vein, such as Jean-Paul Sartre's *Baudelaire* (Paris: Gallimard, 1947), Gaston Bachelard's studies (his *La Poétique de l'espace* was published by PUF in 1957) and the works of Georges Poulet and Jean-Pierre Richard of the so-called Geneva School.

I think there are two sorts of criticism. There is 'launch' criticism, the type expressed in the newspapers and magazines, the aim of which is to inform readers about the value of the books they should or shouldn't buy. This is a criticism that expresses the interests of the reader and fulfils what might be called a hygienic function towards—or provides an economic policing of—literature. Then there is structural criticism, the type expressed in books and learned tomes, which often relates to works from the past and represents a genuine questioning of literature. This isn't about asking the writer: 'How good are you?', but 'Who are you?' and, in a more general and also more unsettling way: 'Deep down, what is literature?'

This structural criticism always consists in re-establishing a relationship between the literary work and something beyond it, which is why we might also call it a functional criticism. This second term of the critical function (that is to say, that which is not the work itself) may be situated, depending on the critical school, in two different—antagonistic—regions of reality. We may say, as Taine and Plekhanov do, that a literary work is the product of a history, a society, a moment and a milieu. Or, conversely, that it is the expression of an inwardness, a psychology. For a very long time now, this alternative has structured the debate within French criticism: we must either choose history, in which case the work and literature vanish and become pure, unqualified ideological reflections; or we must choose the author, and then it is the powerful reality of the historical world that is bracketed out.

Our criticism hasn't yet resolved this contradiction and we may even say that it is becoming more acute by the day. However, what is new and, all in all, encouraging is the fact that on both sides of the argument, points of view are being refined and an increasing number of working hypotheses developed. In short, there is more and more intelligence in evidence, and intelligence is the power in which we should always trust.

For example, in the area of historical criticism, Lucien Goldmann has, in his work *The Hidden God* [1964], managed substantially to refine and enrich the relationship between history and literary works, which was too often presented mechanically in the past. Taking the works of Pascal and Racine as his object and drawing on the work of Lukács on tragedy, he has attempted to introduce a new ideological mediation between the writings of these authors and the society of their time—the tragic vision. On the one hand, he has teased out an identical argument from Pascalian thought and Racinian tragedy: cast out from the worldly circles he condemns and intimidated by a spectator-God who watches him but never speaks, tragic man is up against the impossible—this gives us tragedy. On the other hand, Goldmann has established that Pascal and Racine belonged to the same social group, to that Jansenist milieu whose members came from the *noblesse de robe*, largely recruited from among the functionaries of Louis XIV's early monarchy, the people known as *officiers*.[1] And Goldmann's hypothesis is that, when Louis XIV moved from limited to absolute monarchy, he cleared out the *officiers* and entrusted his administration to a new caste of bureaucrats, the *commissaires*. Goldmann sees Jansenism—particularly on its right wing, that of the theologian Barcos—as the ideology of the ousted group, thwarted in its political aspirations and transforming its disappointment into a genuine tragic vision of the world, in which, as it were, man can justly find no place.

1 The beliefs of the 'Jansenists' derived ultimately from the writings of Dutch theologian Cornelius Jansen (1585–1638). The epithet was applied by Jesuits to Catholics at the Abbaye de Port-Royal de Paris, who were suspected of affinities with Calvinism. Some of the Jansenists' core beliefs were denounced as heretical by Pope Innocent X in 1653. [Trans.]

Standing over against this—happily reinvigo-
rated—historical criticism, there is currently in France
an even more remarkable refinement of psychological
criticism. Properly psychoanalytic criticism does not
come under the heading of literature because, for that
approach, the work of art only ever supplies material
for a diagnosis that aims to define the writer's neurosis.
Racine, Hugo, Baudelaire and Mallarmé have been
analysed through their works in this way; but the most
convincing study in this area, bearing the stamp of its
author's genius, is Freud's analysis of Jensen's *Gradiva*,
because it is the very quality of the novel that is
explained and *conveyed* there, not merely its signification as a product of neurosis.

It is, in fact, the central concern of the new criticism to retain the work's objective and, to some degree,
structured nature. Thus, for example, Sartre in his
highly controversial but most stimulating *Baudelaire*
has sketched out a genuine thematic study of the
Baudelairian universe. Starting out from the hypothesis that Baudelaire conducted his whole life as a *project* of failure, born out of childhood frustration (at the
point when Baudelaire was separated from his mother
who remarried), Sartre has produced some acclaimed
analyses of Baudelairian metaphors of sterility and the
rejection of nature. But it is probably the philosopher
Gaston Bachelard who has so far pushed this depth
criticism furthest. Amassing a considerable quantity
of material from the poets of many nations, he has

reconstructed extensive networks of themes, all those chains of images by which poets transform the original sensation prompted in them by one of the world's major substances—fire, air, earth and water. Bachelard's principle is that the poetic imagination is a power that *undoes* images, and what he studies are not closed, immobile metaphors—ready-made metaphors, as we might say—but genuine lines of development of images. In a series of books devoted to the four elements, Bachelard has described the dynamics of the great poetic themes—for example, the theme of the labyrinth, of flight, ascent, fall, etc. And Bachelard's is a generous criticism, one that helps to produce, within the interiority of one's own body, the very movement of the poetic imagination which is essentially liberating. It is in this same climate, though with substantial individual differences, that other French-language critics such as Georges Poulet or Jean-Pierre Richard also work, the latter having brilliantly analysed our great nineteenth-century writers using an analytic method of this kind (in *Poésie et profondeur* [1955] and *Littérature et sensation* [1954]).

This is a very fine form of criticism, but, like the historical variant, it too is incomplete. It admirably conveys the unity of the work, its quality as an aesthetic object, but tells us nothing of its historical significance. And so we come up against two kinds of failings: either criticism provides an account of history, but, by ideologizing the work of art, de-realizes it; or, it gives an account of the work of art, but, by substantifying it, de-realizes history. For myself, I am convinced that this twofold failure is merely temporary; moreover, it is not unhealthy insofar as this very dilemma (history or *Psyche*) defines literature itself. What, indeed, is a work of art if not both the product of a history and a resistance to that history? In its ambiguity lies the dialectical nature and the greatness of literature. It is a product of its age and yet stands out against it—the literary work is both a *structure* and a *movement*. It is a structure in movement and that is why it is so often difficult to analyse. I am convinced that the current task of criticism is to reconcile in a genuine, living synthesis the as-yet-scattered segments of that total criticism which current demands for scientific explanation place so clearly on the agenda.

A Personal Statement
on Robbe-Grillet

This article appeared in December 1961 in the columns of *Clarté*, the magazine of the Union des Étudiants Communistes [Union of Communist Students], the cultural pages of which were relatively open in this period to discussions of the relative merits of ortho-dox 'committed literature' and a less overtly political avant-garde.

It is one of several texts Barthes devoted to the work of Robbe-Grillet, the most notable of which are probably 'Objective Literature' of 1954 (*Critical Essays*. Evanston: Northwestern University Press, 1972, pp. 13–24), 'Literal Literature' of 1955 (ibid., pp. 51–8) and 'There Is No Robbe-Grillet School' of 1958 (ibid., pp. 91–6). As in the case of the 'Round Table' article, Barthes is more sympathetic here to Robbe-Grillet's literary project than to other aspects of his activity.

Oeuvres complètes, Volume 1, pp. 1116–17

I would happily grant Robbe-Grillet the following: he has cleansed novel-writing of its adjectives and, by that very act, attempted to shake the novel reader out of one of his most complacent habits. A traditional description—the kind that passes without question—is laden with parasitical values: beneath the tyranny of 'good writing' (the use of sophisticated adjectives, metaphorical touches, felicitous turns of phrase, stylistic invention, etc.), things in traditional literature are no longer things but confused objects, situated loosely at the crossroads of multiple consciousnesses, multiple perceptions, multiple memories. Robbe-Grillet has tried to get back to a *possible* function of language, which is to abstract. He hasn't tried to show something— to make us see it (as has been the way in literature for 150 years)—but to make it exist. He has wanted the things in novels simply to *be*, and not to *be something*. He has wanted the sky not to be clear or deep or stormy, but to *be*. Hence a vision based on a pure relation between objects, since only the clear fact of a spatial (and even, in his case, spatial and temporal) function can triumph over the relentless tendency of things to become familiar again by way of an accompanying escort of adjectives.

There wouldn't be any point accusing Robbe-Grillet of writing a reactionary literature on the grounds that his view of the world is a 'de-humanized' one. First, because his vision, without being romantic, is nonetheless perfectly 'human'—it is the eye of a man that constructs this world of objects, no more or less 'projected' than the objects of a painter; and it is the activity of a mind that constructs, if we may put it like that, this 'absence' of significations. And, then again, because literature, at least within the historical scale known to us, is constitutively reactionary—not only because it is removed from all 'doing' but also because it is entirely defined, even within a progressive project, by the construction of essences, the representation of things that *are*, not things that *become*. No, what we may ask of Robbe-Grillet is what he is going to do with this power he has tried to acquire over 'things' or, more exactly, over 'thing-words'. Does he want to carry on making 'texts' or to set about making 'novels'? If he aspires to write novels, then to recount what narrative? How is he thinking of going about it if he is to reconcile narrative and vision? For it is at the level of the subject, the argument, the anecdote that the difficulties begin—the crafting of a 'pure' vision prohibits the recourse to what is a necessarily impure knowledge on the part of the reader. Without 'impurity', there is no 'story', and without a story, there is no novel—merely a verbal composition, analogous to the texts of Mallarmé, not to the works of Stendhal.

But already, it seems, we have Robbe-Grillet's answer: by agreeing to 'make' a film, he, the writer of pure verbal vision, in identifying completely with the cinematic work of Resnais (see the preface to the synopsis of *Last Year in Marienbad*), has chosen to go back to a literature of adjectives, however fine they may be. He who wanted things to *be*—without attributes, appendices or harmonics—sees his *world* here as one that has 'a certain ceremonious solidity, often slow-moving, with a theatrical sense', etc. By telling *one* story—whether of love, death, dreams or adultery matters little—he has opted against all the other stories in the world, thereby permitting us to prefer the world to *that* story. His literature is no longer reactionary in an ontological sense, then, but has become so ideologically.

The Two Sociologies
of the Novel

Barthes had written articles for *Combat* between 1947 and 51 when its literary pages were under the editorship of Maurice Nadeau. With the latter's move to *L'Observateur* (subsequently *France-Observateur*) in 1951, Barthes, just returned from a period as a French *lecteur* in Alexandria, wrote to Nadeau to say that he would like to be able 'to work again for you and with you' and was subsequently invited to produce articles for both *L'Observateur* and *Les Lettres nouvelles*.

This article for *France-Observateur* (5 December 1963) was prompted by the publication, under the auspices of the Université libre de Bruxelles, of the Belgian *Revue de l'Institut de Sociologie* 2 (1963). This issue was produced, according to its Contents page, by the Centre de recherches de sociologie littéraire de l'Institut de Sociologie, of which Lucien Goldmann had been director since January 1961. In his work, Goldmann drew on the theoretical writings of the Hungarian-born Marxist philosopher György Lukács and two chapters from that writer's *Theory of the Novel*, not yet published in French, are translated in this number of the journal which also carries a short

Oeuvres complètes, Volume 2, pp. 248–50

article by René Girard entitled 'De "la divine comédie" à la sociologie du roman' (From 'The Divine Comedy' to the Sociology of the Novel). The articles by Köhler and Bernard mentioned here are entitled, respectively, 'Les romans de Chrétien de Troyes' and 'L'oeuvre romanesque de Malraux vue à travers la presse de l'entre-deux-guerres'.

As with Barthes's earlier round-up of current critical trends (see p. 44), one of his major concerns here is to seek a middle way between two apparently divergent tendencies, so that sociohistorical content is not evacuated as interesting new types of formal analysis are developed.

Some years ago, informed by the work of Lukács, Lucien Goldmann developed a sociology of tragedy or, at least, of the tragic vision. An author equipped with an original method always has a difficult time demonstrating it a second time. But it seems that Goldmann is in the process of pulling off such a demonstration. Drawing, on this occasion, on the analyses of René Girard (in *Mensonge romantique et vérité romanesque*), which coincide, in the main, with those of Lukács, Goldmann is currently working on a sociology of the novel, the guiding principle of which he illustrates in three fragments published together in a special issue of the *Revue de l'institut de sociologie de l'université libre de Bruxelles* entitled 'Problems of a Sociology of the Novel'. Alongside an article by Lukács and some excellent analyses by René Girard, Erich Köhler and Michel Bernard, that publication carries three pieces by Goldmann himself: a general theory of the sociology of the novel; a study of the novels of Malraux; and an article situating the works of Nathalie Sarraute and Alain Robbe-Grillet in sociological terms.

For some time now, critics (or historians) have shown a relationship between literature and society. For the first time, Goldmann, alongside Lukács and Girard, brings a greater specificity to that relationship—he sees the novel as a 'form' (distinct, for example, from the tragic or epic form). What does form mean for Goldmann? It is what others would call content. But since that content is typical and is constant in its generality across an infinity of anecdote, it operates as a formula that is fleshed out by a great variety of storylines. The novel is, in fact, 'the story of a degraded quest for authentic values in an inauthentic world'. That quest is led by a hero whom Lukács terms *demonic* and Goldmann *problematic*. The hero of the novel knows that he is living in an inauthentic world, within which he feels his own authenticity. But (unlike the tragic hero) he does not form a clear awareness of the contradiction itself (and its insolubility). This explains why the hero of the novel has need of a certain sense of community with the world, but is constantly asserting his separation from it (this is the case, it seems, with the great protagonists of novels, from Julien Sorel to Proust's narrator). That protagonist is simultaneously engaged and disengaged. However, a psychological situation is not sufficient in itself to constitute a literary form—that form does not emerge until the novelist detaches himself somewhat from his hero and steps beyond his awareness (or lack of it) by an act of *irony* (Lukács) or *humour* (Girard).

Such is the 'form' of the novel. With that form established (Goldmann also calls it a structure), the question arises of what society it corresponds to and, most importantly, *how* it corresponds to it. It has been suspected for some time now that the novel, in the time of its great flowering, is the privileged genre of capitalist society. And yet this kind of equation, being both vague and mechanical, has always failed to satisfy. Goldmann, it seems, recasts the problem thoroughly by radicalizing it (often a good way of overcoming a methodological impasse); Marxist (or merely historical) criticism always established the relay of a collective consciousness between society and the literary work, a kind of double-sided mirror placed between the economic and the aesthetic structure.

Goldmann eliminates that relay, or at least uses the—at times, present and at others absent—relay to sketch out a typology internal to the 'novel' form. In novels with problematic heroes (the ones Goldmann is chiefly concerned with), economic and novelistic structures coincide directly and immediately, as do the inauthenticity of the world in which the hero lives and the omnipotent reign of an economy in which ('reifying') exchanges-values have supplanted use-values, though the creator and his hero remain attached to these latter. From Stendhal to early Malraux, these types of novel correspond closely to the development of the bourgeoisie but are in no way the expression of bourgeois collective consciousness.

To relocate that relay of collective consciousness (or class consciousness), Goldmann suggests that we posit a second type of novel, such as Balzac's, in which the conscious values of the bourgeoisie (individualism, money, eroticism) constitute the very authenticity of the world and thereby eliminate the problematic hero (the few rare Balzacian heroes, such as Rastignac, are actually in harmony with their society).

Such, simplified in the extreme (as may be suspected), is the sociology of the novel proposed by Goldmann. Do I have reservations about it? This is a project in full flow, deeply intelligent and noble in intent, and one cannot but be carried along by it with no desire to hold back or quibble. But questions arise perhaps—or, at the very least, one question. Criticism is about 'level of perception' and the level Goldmann situates himself at is essentially ideological. What becomes, in this macro-critique, of the verbal *surface* of the work, that perfectly coherent body of formal phenomena (in the most external sense of the term), the styles of writing, the forms of rhetoric, the modes of narration, techniques of perception, criteria of notation that also *make up* the novel? Paradoxically, Goldmann's 'form' seems to allow 'forms' to elude it, as though the literary specificity of the novel were fully accounted for by this passage from abstraction to narrative in which Goldmann takes it to reside.

In other words, the novelist's ethical project, even if we accept the way Goldmann speaks of it (and particularly if we do), must necessarily encounter—*if it is, indeed, to be mediated*—what we shall refer to here as an *imaginary* or, in other words, a *form of language*, and that form of language also has need of its sociology. As a result, we would be inclined today to conceive of two complementary forms of criticism (or sociology): an ideological criticism, which I shall choose to term *semantic*, since it would be concerned with content (which Goldmann calls 'form'); and a *semiological* criticism, because it would concern itself with 'forms'. We might call that sociology of forms a *socio-logic*, insofar as it would attempt to account for the eminently significant way novelists *classify* their words.

Can these two sociologies coexist? Can they, so to speak, go to work together? What we can say is that the second one, being itself an activity of classification, would, I believe, have no difficulty recognizing the importance (if not the truth) of the first.

Alain Girard:
'The Diary'

L'Année sociologique, founded by Émile Durkheim in 1896 and one of France's most prestigious academic journals, published this review of Alain Girard's study *Le Journal Intime* (Paris: PUF, 1963) in 1966. Girard's study examined, among other things, how the emergence of a new type of subjectivity in early-nineteenth-century France went hand in hand with the 'new genre' of the private journal.

Oeuvres complètes, Volume 2, pp. 806–10

The diary is a paradoxical genre. Conceived as the written exercise of the purest, freest subjectivity, and, by its very nature, rejecting all the codifications of the literary work (fiction, construction, fine style) while also remaining indifferent, if not indeed resistant, to publication (at least initially), it is in its very essence a defiance of literature. Though, in its origins, it seemed destined to occupy that narrow window between writing and the literary work as such, under historical and social pressure it very quickly became a literary genre in its own right. The paradox of the diary is precisely that it is a genre. Since that genre combines the most social of things (what can be more social than a published work?) with the most individual (since all the forms of literary work are rejected in this case), it is understandable that the exploration of this paradox should have tempted a sociologist. Understandable and yet felicitous, since literary phenomena do not offer themselves up easily for sociological analysis, which tends to fall short of its object (when it merely studies audiences) or to overshoot it (when it interprets contents). We should therefore be grateful to Alain Girard for having sought to carry out a methodologically balanced analysis of the diary form. His work stands at the point of intersection between literary criticism, sociological analysis and psycho-sociological explanation. Hence the breadth of vision of this study and, if I may put it this way, its great intellectual generosity.

Alain Girard's study is constructed as a triptych: a section that is essentially a monograph analysing the main diaries of the nineteenth century (Maine de Biran, Joubert, Constant, Stendhal, Maurice de Guérin, Vigny, Delacroix, Amiel) is flanked by two more general ones. The first of these is a sociology of the genre in which the author defines the diary in relation to adjacent genres (daily chronicles, memoirs, confessions, reminiscences, correspondence, notebooks, commonplace books and *romans personnels*[1]) and tidies up the chronology of the genre, which emerged around 1800, dividing it into three major

---

1 The *roman personnel* is a recognized subgenre of the French Romantic novel, characterized chiefly by the fictional transposition of the author's life experience. There is some disagreement about precisely which novels belong in the category, but such works as Châteaubriand's *Atala* and *René*, Constant's *Adolphe*, Musset's *La Confession d'un enfant du siècle* and Nerval's *Sylvie* are usually included. [Trans.]

periods. From 1800 to 1860, authors wrote their diaries for their own benefit, without having publication as an ulterior motive (this is the main period studied by Alain Girard). From 1860 to around 1910, the first published diaries ensured the success of this widely practiced genre—the author did not publish his diary yet, but he knew it would eventually be published. From 1910 to the present, the genre has been a thriving one. Scholars have published complete editions (where possible) of early diaries and authors themselves have published their diaries during their lifetimes. This history is completed (in a highly valuable section) by a sociology of the *intimistes*, covering their geographical origins (they were generally provincials facing the problem of adapting to life in Paris), social origins (from among a bourgeoisie that was entirely satisfied with government action), parental situation (premature death of the mother), religious education (Catholic or Protestant, but leaving the individual not fully integrated into a definite religious system), family status (normal marriages, in which, however, the wife remains in the background, except in the case of Michelet, as though there were a kind of rivalry between diary and spouse), profession (the *intimiste* is often unsuccessful socially), physical constitution (they are relatively short-lived) and character (the sentimental type is dominant—emotional, inactive, secondary). This list shows the care taken by Alain Girard in identifying the sociological facts of the *intimiste* experience which commonly takes place within a general climate of failure and frustration (naturally, such a generalization requires nuancing at various points, as Girard never fails to point out).

I have used the term *sociological facts* but it remains to be seen how the individual himself relates to these facts. This is what Girard examines in the third part of his work. What we have here is a psycho-sociology of the *intimiste*, built around the notion of the person, which has always been of great interest to sociologists and ethnologists. What are the *lived* relations between diary-writing and age (and adolescence, in particular)? How does it relate to loneliness, happiness, the body, memory, the sense of guilt and madness? What are the functions of the diary for the person writing it (therapeutic, ethical, aesthetic, religious)? In this way Alain Girard gradually pins down what we might term the *existentiality* of the diary, which certainly constitutes its specific feature; it is sufficient to recall, with Girard, that resistance to diary-writing has mainly come on rationalist, intellectualist or confessional grounds. That existentiality is entirely defined by a certain relation to others—the sense of failure is a social feeling, Girard reminds us, very aptly employing that formulation from social psychology to show how intimism is, in its way, a social behaviour, the function of which is to provide the subject with a substitutive image of the work [*oeuvre*]—the diary is the product of a generalized doubt, but insofar as that doubt is *written*, it is already action.

Apart from its strictly sociological interest, Alain Girard's book makes a substantial contribution (in terms of materials and some very insightful remarks) to a discipline that is, in fact, unknown in France but already well established among the Germans and Anglo-Saxons, which we might call the theory of literature. In other words, many of Girard's observations relate to that question which historians of literature here in France regard as the province of philosophers: What is literature? From among many pertinent remarks, I shall cite two important suggestions here, because they seem to be of topical interest. Girard notes (page *xiv*) that writing has assumed an increasingly prominent place in our society but that, paradoxically, a corollary of this development has been a growing sense of its extreme difficulty. If a universal history of literature were to deal with our age, it might well call that chapter 'The Difficulty of Writing'. The *intimistes* are clearly the first to attest to that difficulty. Once again, the private diary helps us to understand this generalized *mauvaise conscience* among modern writers, which is no doubt linked to the ideological history of the bourgeoisie. Criticism could also usefully consider another remark made by Alain Girard to the effect that the desire to wrest its 'secret' from the private diary at all costs should be resisted. Is there ultimately a 'secret' of the individual? The real problem for criticism is not to arrive at knowledge of the hidden motive behind a life (since the life of the *intimiste* is, all in all, his work)—that would be an illusory pursuit, since human beings are obscure as a result of complexity, not secrecy—but, rather, to find the meaning an author is able to give to the ceaseless quest that is writing. In other words, when faced with any piece of private writing (and perhaps with any literary work), the question is not 'What is the author hiding from us?' but 'Why is he writing?' This is a valuable methodological comment that ought to take away from literary criticism the temptation to regard itself as seeking to discover a hidden truth or, in short, to be a hermeneutics.

Alain Girard's work mainly covers the first *intimistes*, from Maine de Biran to Amiel. Though the genre is still a thriving one in terms of readers' interest, we may venture the idea that literature today (at least the literature pursuing new forms) no longer regards it very highly. It is mainly writers from an already ageing generation (François Mauriac, Julien Green) who still keep diaries. As frequently happens, it is at the point when a genre is widely accepted by the public that it comes into crisis with creative writers. This idea would probably call for a further work of research, which would have to draw on the situation of our literature as a whole, since literary genres can less and less be treated separately, given the number of current texts that cannot be apportioned to any definite genre. We should no doubt pick out two distinct lines of evolution here. On the one hand, the diary as defined by Alain Girard has become impossible (I mean among the new creative writers) and the reason for this is very clear (and entirely corroborates the link established by

Girard between the diary and the notion of person)—
the *self* can no longer tell its story because it is no
longer recognized as an entity (however difficult to
grasp that entity might have seemed to the *intimistes*).
What is *I*? No avant-garde writer would be willing
to answer that question ('Kill oneself? But who kills
himself, if he kills himself? Who kills one*self*? What
is 'who' in all that?' writes Philippe Sollers in his latest
novel *Drame*). Admittedly, it is not now for reasons
of morality or aesthetics that the writer no longer
speaks of himself in the first person. It is because the
self no longer has the status of a psychological object.
Confronted with the problematic of the person, under-
mined by private diary-writing, contemporary literature, at least in the form of its avant-garde, regards
experiences of depersonalization as established truth.
On grounds clearly contrary to his, contemporary
writers could, in opposing diary-writing, take over
Aristotle's commandment that men should neither
speak of themselves nor of others. And, in fact, this
allows current literature to bracket out the problem of
sincerity, the positive crux of diary writing, as Alain
Girard emphasizes several times in his book.

However, if the *intimisme* of the diary is impossible
today, there is another of its features that is enjoying a
considerable vogue, and that is *reflexivity*. By this I
mean writing's power to reflect on itself. Our literature
is increasingly a literature that talks about literature, a
language expressing itself about language, pondering
what conditions make it possible and deriving from

that dizzying game new truths in harmony with the discoveries of psychoanalysis and linguistics. There can be no doubt that the diary, psychologistic as it may now seem, is at the origin of this *reflection* (if we take the word in its optical rather than mental sense). If diary writing is no longer practised by the new writers, that is in some degree because all their texts are formed out of an observation of language, which is a kind of diary even if their observations are no longer recorded on a daily basis. All in all, diaries and current texts could both take as their motto this remark by Pascal (I quote from memory): 'I had a thought; I've forgotten it; I write, instead, that I've forgotten it.'[2] The diary, which bears the strong imprint of a psychology of the person and of the desire to escape, in a way, from literature, is ultimately just the initial moment in a history that leads today to a depersonalized literature. By shedding such perfect light on that moment, Alain Girard enables us better to read the vast dialectic that unites contemporary writers with their past.

2 Barthes would seem to have in mind here the text that appears as fragment 100 of Pascal's *Pensées* in the 1954 Pléiade edition of the *Oeuvres complètes*. This particular section is rendered as follows in the Trotter translation of 1958, where it figures as fragment 372: 'In writing down my thought, it sometimes escapes me; but this makes me remember my weakness, that I constantly forget. This is as instructive to me as my forgotten thought; for I strive only to know my nothingness.' [Trans.]

Parallel Lives

Oeuvres complètes, Volume 2, pp. 811–13

The following piece, published in *La Quinzaine littéraire* (15 March 1966), is a review of the French translation of the first volume of George D. Painter's biography of Proust, *Marcel Proust 1871–1903: les années de jeunesse* (Paris: Mercure de France, 1966). The English original was published as *Marcel Proust: a Biography*, Volume I (London: Chatto & Windus, 1959).

La Quinzaine littéraire, which became one of France's major literary magazines, was launched in 1966 by Maurice Nadeau and François Erval, who also worked with Nadeau at the Éditions Robert Marin. Barthes contributed occasional articles to the journal in its early years.

The work referred to here simply as *A la recherche* is, of course, Proust's *A la recherche du temps perdu*. This was initially translated into English as *Remembrance of Things Past* (by C. K. Scott-Moncrieff and Terence Kilmartin), though more recent translations have adopted the title *In Search of Lost Time*.

Nothing, on the face of it, predisposes Proust's life to major biographical treatment. It wasn't an adolescent (Rimbaud), adventurous (Byron), titanic (Balzac) or tragic (Van Gogh) life. It was the life of a socialite who was both idle and rich (and we know how suspicious we are today of writers' money), and its backdrop, divided between Haussmann's Paris and Normandy, is a period of bourgeois history commonly—and ironically—referred to as *la belle époque* and more often the subject of films than the substance of literature. And yet it turns out that Proust's life is fascinating, as is attested by the success of Painter's book and the intense and even peculiar pleasure we find in it. Why is this?

No doubt Proust's work already has some sort of direct relationship with the biographical genre, since that unique and comprehensive literary work is the narrative of a life that runs from childhood to writing, with the result that Marcel and his narrator are a bit like those heroes of Antiquity that Plutarch paired together in his *Parallel Lives*. But a first paradox arises at this point, though, all in all, a disappointing one:

taken extensively (and not in their substance), the parallel lives of Proust and his narrator intersect only very rarely. What the two have in common is a very basic set of events or, rather, structural articulations: a long period of life in fashionable society, an intense bout of mourning (over mother or grandmother), an involuntary withdrawal (to a sanatorium) and a deliberate severance from life (the cork-lined room) for the purpose of elaborating the literary work. These common points occupy the same position in the time period of the work or the life, but it must be admitted that they don't have anything like the same role. The death of his mother marked a crucial divide in Proust's life; the death of the grandmother changes nothing of the narrator's existence and all the grieving for her is delegated to his mother (an enigmatic substitution worthy of some reflection). Moreover, Proust's involuntary withdrawal from life is very short (a few weeks at a clinic in Boulogne) whereas the narrator's (in *Time Regained*) is extremely long, since he subsequently discovers a world that has, strangely, donned the mask of old age. All things considered, between the lived life and the written life, there is no analogy but merely homology. We have here two outlines that definitely seem to be linked by a certain relationship of allusion, but that relationship remains opaque—it is either too clear or too deep. So where does the riddle of these two parallel lives come from? To restate the point: Why can we read Proust's life with the kind of eagerness with which we 'devour' a story?

The truth is that, most paradoxically, Proust's life obliges us to *critique* the use we normally make of biographies. We usually take the view that a writer's life ought to provide information about his work and try to find a sort of causal link between the adventures in his life and the episodes in his narrative, as though the former produced the latter. We believe that the biographer's labour authenticates the literary work, which seems 'truer' to us if we can be shown that it was lived, so tenaciously do we cling to the prejudice that art is ultimately illusion and that we must, at every possible opportunity, lend it the substance of a little reality, a little contingency. Now, Proust's life obliges us to reverse this prejudice—it isn't Proust's life we find in his work but *Proust's work we find in his life*. To read Painter's book (which has the virtue of extreme transparency) is not to discover the origins of *A la recherche* but to read a duplicate of the novel, as though Proust had written the same work twice—once in his book and once in his life. We do not get the impression (at least this is the way I felt) that Montesquiou is clearly the model for Charlus but, on the contrary, that there is something of Charlus in Montesquiou, something of Balbec in Cabourg, something of Albertine in Agostinelli.

In other words (at least in the case of Proust), it isn't the life that informs the work but the work that radiates out and explodes into the life, scattering into it the thousand fragments that seem to pre-exist it. Doäzan, Lorrain, Montesquiou and Wilde don't *make up* Charlus, but Charlus is scattered in—and forming in—these few real figures, whose number is variable, though each new biography impishly adds to it. This paradoxical reading is consonant with what we can glimpse of Proust's philosophy (particularly since Gilles Deleuze's book *Proust and Signs*). The Proustian world is a Platonic world (much more than it is Bergsonian); it is populated with essences and it is these essences that are scattered around Proust's work and life—the essence fragments without deteriorating and the undiminished elements find their way into phenomena that may be fictional or may be real (ultimately, it does not matter which).

We understand then how pointless it is to seek out 'keys' to *A la recherche*. The world doesn't provide keys to the book, it is the book that opens up the world. Admittedly, Proust's life itself provides a favoured field for the scattering of those essences, but it is not the only possible one. Each of our individual lives may open itself up to receive Proustian essences. Hence the constant feeling of running into Proust's world in our own lives (the way that Swann encountered Giotto's Charity or Rizzo's Doge Loredan in the kitchen maid with the asparagus or his coachman Rémi). Who does not still, in 1966, come across Monsieur de Norpois expatiating on literature or Octave–'I'm a washout', an uneducated young man but one well versed in the world of bars, sport and fashion? Proust's truth comes not from an inspired copying of reality but a philosophical reflection on essences and art. Hence, despite the paradox, when the reader reads Proust's life not as coming before his work but as coming after it, it is he who is right and not the critic who attempts to explain Proust's work through his life.

We may put this biographical paradox a different way: the lives of Marcel and the narrator are two planes available for the dispersal of the same essences. But what is not parallel between them, because it is a single, merged, identical thing, is the writing—that is where the parallels meet. When Marcel shuts himself up in his cork-lined room, he does so to write; when the narrator bids the world farewell (at the Guermantes matinee), he does so finally to begin his book. In other words, it is only then that the two parallel lives indissolubly meld their timescales together—the narrator's writing is, word for word, Marcel's writing: there is neither author nor character, but only a writing.

Pleasure in Language

Oeuvres complètes, Volume 2, pp. 1238–40

This further contribution to *La Quinzaine littéraire* (15 May 1967) was Barthes's third, since he had also reviewed Émile Benveniste's *Problèmes de linguistique générale*, Volume 1, in May 1966. It is a review of the Cuban writer Severo Sarduy's experimental novel *Écrit en dansant* (Paris: Seuil, 1967), the French translation of *De dónde son las cantantes*. The book has been translated into English by Suzanne Jill Levine as *From Cuba with a Song* (Los Angeles: Sun & Moon Press, 1994).

Barthes also alludes in this piece to Sarduy's first novel *Gestos* (1963).

French culture has, it seems, always attached very great significance to 'ideas' or, to put it more neutrally, to the content of messages. What is important to the French is the *quelque chose à dire*—that 'something' writers have 'to say', commonly referred to by a word that is phonically ambiguous and has meanings extending across the monetary, commercial and literary fields: *le fond* ('content', akin in its sound to *le fonds*, 'business' or 'fund', and *les fonds*, 'funds' or 'capital'). In terms of the signifier (a term I hope we can now use without having to apologize for it), French culture for years knew only stylistic endeavour, the constraints of Aristotelo-Jesuit rhetoric, and the values of 'fine writing', which were themselves focused—and here the same requirement returns stubbornly—on the transparency and distinction of the *fond* or 'content'. Not until Mallarmé's arrival on the scene did our literature develop the idea of a free signifier that no longer had the censure of the false signified hanging over it and ventured upon the experiment of a writing at last rid of the historical repression imposed on it by the superior demands of 'thought'. And so keen is the resistance that even the Mallarmean enterprise can only be 'varied' here and there—that is to say, repeated—by way of some rare works that are always combative endeavours. Stifled twice in our history, first at the upsurge of the baroque and then at the point when Mallarmean poetics emerged, French writing is still in a repressed state.

A book has appeared which reminds us that, outside of cases of transitive or moral communication ('Pass me the cheese' or 'We sincerely wish for peace in Vietnam'), there is a pleasure of language that is of the same—silky—substance as erotic pleasure, and that this pleasure of language is its truth. This book doesn't come from Cuba (this is not about folklore, even Castroite folklore) but from the language of Cuba, from that Cuban text (towns, words, drinks, clothes, bodies, odours, etc.) that is itself the inscription of diverse cultures and times. Now, something is going on here that is of importance to us as French people: when transported into French, this Cuban language subverts the landscape of our own. This is one of the very rare times when a translation manages to displace its language of origin instead of merely connecting with it. Though the verbal baroque is, in historical terms, Spanish (it is Gongoresque or Quevedian) and though that history is present in Severo Sarduy's text, which like any 'mother' tongue is national and 'maternal', that text also discloses the baroque aspect to be found in the French idiom, thereby suggesting that writing can do anything with a language—not least, give it back its freedom.

Insofar as it displays the ubiquity of the signifier, which is present at all levels of the text and not just, as is commonly argued, at its surface, this baroqueness (a term that is useful in a provisional way for challenging French literature's deep-rooted classicism) modifies the very identity of what we call a narrative, without the pleasure of the tale ever being lost. *Écrit en dansant* [*De dónde son las cantantes*] is made up of three episodes, three *gestos*—the Spanish title of Sarduy's first book, which we can understand here to mean both act or gesture and tale of heroic exploits—but none of the narrative prostheses (personalities of the protagonists, geographical and temporal settings, authorial winks and nods, and God seeing into the heart of the characters) are to be found there by which we ordinarily mark the improperly ascribed (and indeed illusory) rights of reality over language. Sarduy does indeed narrate 'something', which draws us on towards its end and moves in the direction of the death of writing, but that something is freely displaced, 'led astray' by that *sovereignty* of language which Plato was already eager to impugn in the hands of a Gorgias, thereby inaugurating the repression of writing that marks our Western culture. And so we see deployed in *Écrit en dansant*, a hedonistic and hence revolutionary text, the major theme proper to the signifier, the only predicate of essence it can truly bear, which is metamorphosis:

Severo Sarduy's creatures, whether Cuban, Chinese, Spanish, Catholic, drug-addicted, theatrical or pagan, travelling from caravels to cafeterias and from one sex to the other, move back and forth through the windows of a refined chatter which they also 'foist' on the author, thereby demonstrating that that window doesn't exist, that there is nothing to be seen *behind* language and that, far from being the final attribute of—and the last touch to—the human statue, as the illusory myth of Pygmalion tells us, the Word is only ever solidly coterminous with it.

However, let humanists be reassured—at least to some extent. The allegiance paid to writing by any subject, the one who writes and the one who reads— an act that bears no relation to what classical repression in its self-interested ignorance calls 'verbalism' or, more nobly, 'poetry'—suppresses none of the 'pleasures' of reading, provided we are willing to find the right rhythm. Severo Sarduy's text is worthy of all the adjectives in the lexicon of literary value: it is a brilliant, lively, sensitive, funny, inventive, unexpected text and yet, at the same time, it is clear, cultural even and unfalteringly warm-hearted. However, I fear that, to gain easy acceptance in good literary society, it lacks that touch of remorse, that hint of wickedness, that shadow of a signified that transforms writing into a lesson and thereby reclaims it, under the name of 'fine literary work', as a commodity that can serve in the economy of the 'human'. Perhaps this text also has an excessive

·element that will prove troublesome—verbal energy, which is sufficient for the writer to feel at ease with himself.

Edoardo Sanguineti

Oeuvres complètes, Volume 2, pp. 1241–2

The following text was published in the May 1967 edition of the catalogue of Milanese publisher Feltrinelli entitled *100 narratori di Feltrinelli*. It did not appear in French until its inclusion in Barthes's Complete Works. Edoardo Sanguineti was a prominent and prolific literary figure in Italy, one of the leading lights of the 'neo-avant-gardist' Gruppo 63 movement, alongside such writers as Giorgio Manganelli, Umberto Eco and Nanni Ballestrini. Between 1979 and 1983, he was also a deputy in the Italian parliament as an independent with Communist affiliations. Though he is not much translated into English, two of Sanguineti's works have been translated into French by Jean Thibaudeau for the Tel Quel collection of the Éditions du Seuil (*Capriccio italiano*, 1963, and *Le Noble Jeu de l'oye*, 1967). This is despite the fact that many of the leading figures around the Tel Quel group—Michel Foucault in particular—had shown themselves to be fiercely at odds with his Marxist realism at the 1963 Cerisy Colloquium on the theme of 'A New Literature?'

We have a new state of affairs to contend with today, which emerged with the writings of Marx: the capitalist world, the moral world—our world—is, literally, *contemptible*. It is to be rejected. Marxism has placed on our path the monumental stone of rejection, which no writer can evade, roll away or circumvent. Admittedly, literature, which is critical in its essence, has always expressed what is 'wrong with' the world. However, since the disclosure effected by Marxism (which is not reformist but revolutionary— that is to say, total), it is the very form the writer uses which, sooner or later, will have to be absorbed into his critique of the world: the language in which one rejects, coming from the very world that one rejects, must itself also be rejected. It is as a function of this crucial difficulty, apparently, that every modern work must be read, examined, evaluated and loved.

Holding in a single hand (in a single form of writing) the world that is to be destroyed, the destruction of that world, and the destruction of that destruction (since what destroys is unfalteringly complicit with what is destroyed), Edoardo Sanguineti contrives his literary work from just that impossible circuit: on the one hand, he rejects realist art, ever happy to describe capitalist subjection in the very language of bourgeois order; and, on the other, he liberates, explores words and images, mixes poetic meanings and novelistic genres in what seems a classic avant-gardist venture. But the liberation isn't naively positive here; it has something convoluted and inverted about it— in a word, something dialectical. The linguistic and imaginative babelism that Sanguineti contrives aims to copy the profound chaos of the neo-capitalist world in parodic mode; at the same time, that language cannot achieve such disorder without liberating something previously unknown; hence, through a critical baroqueness, a liberating descent into the crucible (or should we say, hell?) of primal senses, essential images, unconscious figures and connections that are variously alchemical, erotic and oneiric. In this way Sanguineti produces a doubled-up writing (a duplicitous writing) which ironizes order but also disorders irony, destroys rhetoric but also exalts the rhetorical figure—it is a carnivalesque, 'Menippean' writing, as Bakhtin puts it, since it merrily substitutes for the terroristic syllogism of bourgeois society the transfinite sequences of a two-track logic that is as yet unknown, except, precisely, to the great precursors.

That being the case, Sanguineti belongs to that very small group of truly audacious writers who, in seeking the truth of their world (which isn't just any old world) in the parodic explosion of forms, have at last shattered the (good) conscience and (bad) faith of proudly progressive literature: in staking their all on writing, in reducing once again, to use Dante's expression—to which Sanguineti himself alludes—the distance between *dir* and *fatto*, they are at last writing the revolutionary literature of a non-revolutionary world.

Preface

(Encyclopédie Bordas, Volume VIII: L'Aventure littéraire de l'humanité I)

Oeuvres complètes, Volume 3, pp. 627–31

This essay was the preface to Volume VIII of the prestigious *Bordas Encyclopaedia*, a volume subtitled 'Humanity's Literary Adventure, I' (Paris: Éditions Bordas, 1970). Bordas, founded in 1946, is a prominent publisher of reference works and school textbooks.

An encyclopaedia is usually thought of as a work of learning. But what counts as learning where literature is concerned? If the physical sciences can change and sometimes disprove their own teachings, varying in different periods and societies, then naturally the same applies to an even greater degree to literary science. The definitions of heat and light may vary, but these phenomena can at least be dealt with in an orderly way through their effects which are constant and hence observable, calculable and explicable. The literary text, by contrast, is not a phenomenon and it would be absurd to try to study it through its effects. We know with certainty what happens if we remove a person's liver, but what would happen if we excised *The Divine Comedy* or *Ulysses* from the social body? It would no doubt be regrettable, but how would the damage *work itself out*? To tell the truth, we are less and less clear about how to define literature. Should we do so by its *structure*—that is to say, by the combination of a content and a form? That division is itself seriously disputed: getting to the bottom of a literary work is an endless task, with 'content' forever eluding our grasp, and modern techniques of analysis only ever revealing new *forms* of content. Should we base ourselves on its—anthropological or social—*function*? But that function is uncertain and we are none too sure today that literature merely serves to instruct, entertain or even express, represent and reflect. No teleological justification is to be found—perhaps literature has no purpose whatever. Should we look to its—aesthetic, moral or philosophical)—value? For a long time we believed (and this is still taught today) that literature was one of the 'noble' institutions of literate societies, one of the major forms of humanism, like religion and art. But modernity has tended to detach the literary from the human (which is denounced as a mystification) and see texts, poems, writing or theatre as ranking alongside the most subversive acts humanity can dare to perform. Like the Argo of Greek legend, which retained the same name despite all its parts having been replaced at one time or another, literature is ultimately merely a stable name for a ceaselessly elusive swirl of concepts, forms and experiences.

For want of a better approach, we have, for a little more than a century now, reduced this—impossible—literary knowledge to a form of historical learning, since history has managed to become a science. People write 'histories of literature', that history is taught in schools and it has entered so-called mass culture (biographical novels, TV quizzes, etc.). Yet that history is itself very much pared down—it is a history that is, so to speak, homogeneous and self-referential. It is, in a nutshell, *based on filiation*, establishing lineages of identical objects (authors, works, schools) which seem, as a result, to engender one another in a steady progression, provided genius effects a few 'leaps' from time to time. As soon as you try to relate this specific history to history in general—and we know today that we cannot conceive the historical totality without grasping its economic, social base—enormous difficulties arise. Just to confine ourselves to European society, what has been—and is now—the economic function of literature? What type of commodity is a literary work, a poem? Why do we trade these things? What are the relations between literary production (what writers produce) and the class in power? They are no doubt ambiguous, since literature is very often both servile and oppositional, but that dialectic has only rarely been explored up to now. Generally speaking, it seems very difficult to locate the literary phenomenon—a very broad one, since it runs from the production of a commodity to the structure of an object—within a chain of causation: we can describe literature but we cannot explain it. In this sense, we might say that for the scholar it remains as determinate as matter; and just as the most recent theories in physics have gone so far as to undermine the very concept of determination and filiation, so literature—or, at least, its theory—cannot help but undermine the concepts of history and origins, for which reason, indeed, it is still cautiously excluded from the so-called human sciences.

If literature resists its incorporation into the body of learning, as being either too broad or too inconsequential, there is no doubt a very simple logical reason for this: literature itself is a form of learning. If we tot up mentally all the knowledge expressed, mobilized and assembled at all levels by the works of our literature, the resulting mass is enormous and positively encyclopaedic. Like the joker in a pack of cards that can stand in for any other card as required, literature can substitute itself for each of the human sciences. It can be, by turns, sociology, economics, linguistics, geography, history and political science. And that encyclopaedic power is not reserved for humanity's great emblematic works, such as Balzac's *Comédie humaine*, Goethe's *Faust* or the plays of Shakespeare. A poem by Apollinaire, a satire by Swift, a play by Brecht—each of these works, because it is a *text*, an experience of language, necessarily contains a 'crazily' ramifying knowledge, since it comes to us from more than one cultural field and branches off in several directions. The literary work is always a compendium of knowledge (if we include, of course, in knowledge, the errors that help it to advance).

The illusion is that this knowledge isn't 'scientific'. First of all, literary knowledge doesn't take any of the canonical sciences of modern civilization—the mathematical or the experimental—as its model: it is an 'impure', diffuse, rebellious and sometimes parodic knowledge that escapes the constraints of logical principles, but which, by that very token, can remind us that the image we have of science, however dominant and fertile, is nonetheless timebound. In times and societies when science wasn't separated from myth (in the days of the Pre-Socratics or the Middle Ages), literature had a fully fledged epistemological function. The works of Dante represented the very knowledge of the age, a knowledge forced underground with the advent of Galilean science; we might say that since that time literature has been the *dark* science, the science on the fringes of reason that freely mingles with myth, fantasy and humanity's limit-experiences. Since then, this literary knowledge has not expressed itself in the form of 'scientific' discourse.

As we know, no language is free; each obeys a code. To speak or write is necessarily and immediately to submit oneself to a particular code of utterance. The code of science is known for the tightness of its constraints: impersonality, rationality, translucency of form in relation to content, etc. Admittedly, literary language is also subject to a code or, in other words, a set of rules that make it clearly recognizable, but that code is multiple; it deliberately mingles and blurs several styles and is happy to imitate, plagiarize and switch from one form of language to another without warning. This is what has been called the 'carnivalesque' mission of literary language, which the periods of pure classicism have had the greatest difficulty in containing. Putting it another way, we might say that the great difference between scientific and literary knowledge is that, in the case of the former, language is only ever an instrument of communication, whereas, with the latter, that same language is much more broadly a field of significations. In other words, science ('scientific' science) does not attempt to meditate on its own discourse whereas literature constitutes itself always as a discourse on discourse, as a critique of language. It includes its own enunciation in the problems it confronts. We can say, therefore, that it is no longer akin to scientistic science but to modern science, the science which assumes, in its fundamental approach, the infinite relativity of its points of reference. Let us say, a little provocatively, that scientific knowledge is perhaps about to find itself in the same position as literary discourse: above and beyond the algorithms of science and the stylistic affectations of literature, a single dramatism is laying hold of human discourse which is increasingly being forced to think about itself at the very point where it wants to think about the world.

One then understands why any form of knowledge that takes literature as its object is inevitably disappointing—it can only be one body of knowledge dealing with another, and, if it aims to abide by the constraints of science (as currently understood), this second, off-set body of knowledge is necessarily reductive. It *fails to connect with* literature, it fails to grasp that pluralism which produces all that is special about literary practice (reading or writing) and makes it irreplaceable. To correct this failing, there is only one solution: for the critic, historian or scholar to include his own discourse in the object he is dealing with—namely, literature; for him to become, in a word, a writer himself.

In these—apparently negative—conditions, what can the function of a literary encyclopaedia be? Everything becomes clearer, I think, if we accept a distinction between the singularity of knowledge in general and the plurality of objects of knowledge. An encyclopaedia isn't a book of knowledge in general but of specific objects of knowledge. It doesn't provide a powerful system capable of embracing all literary phenomena in exhaustive laws, predictions or analyses. It has no epistemological pretensions. Its truth lies in the *measured* nature of its work. It accepts from the outset the fragmented, heteroclite—in a word, *plural*—character of the information it offers. If it orders this information, then it does so solely to satisfy the current conditions of reading, inherited from our rhetorical education.

It is a judicious and, for that very reason, courageous enterprise in that it has to fulfil several functions at once. Some of these are very minor and even trivial (reminding us of a date, for example) while others may be rather breathtaking in their scope, since the tiniest item of information may suddenly connect with a weighty metaphysical problem and impinge keenly, though quite unexpectedly, on the ideological sensibilities of the reader.

It is this undifferentiated plurality of uses that a good encyclopaedia must accept. The present one, as I see it, adequately fulfils this many-sided mission. As a reader, I have found in it a set of 'services' or, if you prefer, functions that make it useful. It performs, first, a *memory* function with regard to the whole of French literature, learnt at school but then forgotten or, worse, incompletely erased, with the result that the literary map we have in our heads, produced by our forgetting, confusion and misconceptions, is quite simply wrong. Second, it performs an *information* function, since we French people know very little of foreign literature. Third, it performs a *connective* function: by generalizing here and there and by synthesizing, the Encyclopaedia invites comparisons with other fields of scholarship and opens the reader up to the totality of the world (reading the volume devoted to *The Laws of Nature*, I was struck in the most exciting way by certain similarities between the scientific and literary approaches, between Mendeleev's classification and the discoveries of linguistics, between relativity and some perspectives within the latest forms of structuralism, between the 'bootstrap' theory [Chew and Mandelstam] and the current conception of the text, of 'writing'). And, lastly, there is an *evaluative* function: the author of the Encyclopaedia, speaking necessarily from a certain time and a certain place in the world, redistributes the values of literature as a function of that time and place—he identifies prejudices, criticizes received opinions, corrects overestimations and brings little-known works to the fore. He has a hand in that uninterrupted battle of values that has characterized the modern world since it ceased to be feudal and theological, a battle that has had literature, which is the subject of this volume, as its dazzling theatre.

Preface
(*Jacques Prévert*, Fatras)

Oeuvres complètes, Volume 4, p. 170

This short text served as the preface to the 'Collection Folio' reprint of the popular French poet Jacques Prévert's collection of interrelated poems and collages *Fatras* (Paris: Gallimard, 1972). Prévert was known as both a prominent screenwriter and a very popular poet. His book *Paroles*, referred to in the text, was first published by Le Point du Jour in 1946.

'Fatras' means jumble or hotchpotch. The 'Adonis flower' or 'blooddrop' referred to in the second paragraph (French *adonide*) is probably more commonly known in English as 'pheasant's eye'.

Poetry can emerge from images just as easily as it can from words, particularly with someone like Prévert who, being primarily a man of the cinema, has a very sharp sense of the image and its powers of suggestion. *Fatras* stages a confrontation between these two means of expression, with some of the 'collages' Jacques Prévert has been working at for many years reproduced in the book, as if to extend the essential themes of his poetic *oeuvre* into the visual realm.

Those themes, which might be boiled down to a single one—exposing the fraud generated by certain watchwords of our society (above all, the fraud of war, a spectre now at large as never before in our world)—are to be found here in the texts of *Fatras*, penned by the author of *Paroles* in the 1960s. Above all, perhaps, we find them in the little 'Graffiti' and 'Adonis flowers' (it is no accident that this flower is also known as blooddrops), in which substantive truths are conveyed through the puns he is so fond of. Rapid, striking *aperçus* that have become, in recent years, one of his preferred forms of thought and writing. They exude a poetry and a morality with a sort of easy naturalness.

Texts and images are working towards the same goal—to break up the sequences of our habits of thought, rectify daily life, and give that little nudge to commonplaces and conventions that upturns the whole landscape and casts doubt on its rightness.

Argument and Prospectus: A Letter to Philippe Roger

The following letter was written on the publication of Philippe Roger's *Sade, la philosophie dans le pressoir* (Paris: Grasset, Collection 'Figures', 1976) and published in *Les Nouvelles littéraires* on 10 June 1976. Barthes's own *Sade, Fourier, Loyola* had been published by Éditions du Seuil (Collection Tel Quel) in 1971. Roger went on to write one of the first major studies of Barthes's work to appear after his death: *Roland Barthes, Roman* (Paris: Bernard Grasset, 1986).

The Pier Paolo Pasolini film to which Barthes refers here is *Salò o le 121 giornate di Sodoma* of 1975. He reviewed the film in *Le Monde* on 16 June 1976.

Oeuvres complètes, Volume 4, pp. 942–3

29 May 1976

Dear Philippe Roger,

I believe you have written a book on Sade that is *accurate* [*juste*] in the course it takes. Let me explain why I choose this unusual word.

As you know, I had always thought that literary criticism ought to be free (in its method), since there is no *true* meaning of a work, unless the truth of a work is improperly identified with the letter of the text, its origin or its history, etc. Admittedly, critics can't say just 'anything whatever', because we write with the desire of the reader (and the desire for readers) and there is no 'anything whatever' in desire. But they can say a lot of things—criticism is plural. There are, however, some very rare authors who quite properly encroach on that freedom and force us to speak accurately about what they have written. Take a Brecht play—*Mother Courage*, for example. *Mother Courage* has something to say (war alienates its victims to the point where they are even blinded about war itself) and that particular something has to be said by the person who directs *Mother Courage*. There's no way of sidestepping its lesson (or, if you do sidestep it, that's simply a great shame and some pleasure is lost—the pleasure to be had from demonstrating Brecht's point).

I think Sade is, for quite other reasons (obviously), one of these inflexible authors. What he is resistant over is that he wants to show something and stubbornly does so. What does he want to show? A virtue—the virtue of fantasy. His work merely reproduces, in magnified form, a particular scene he laid out in *Juliette* which you will recall: Juliette advises the beautiful Comtesse de Donis not to organize an orgy unless she has first written it out at night by candlelight, as the imagination of desire dictates the episodes to her. And if what the libertine writes is dictated by fantasy, then it is the same with Sade—his writing is dictated by fantasy and we (who rewrite Sade) should never stray from that dictation either to one side or the other. We should never draw him towards the 'real' (as Pasolini unfortunately did in his fine film).

Here, as it seems to me, is what is *accurately judged* in Sade, like the beam of a sensitive balance that must never be made to lean towards 'philosophy' or towards 'pornography' but must have its needle pointing always towards what is, as I see it, the only *value* Sade's production knows—namely, writing. It is significant that what modern criticism (no doubt dealing with the most urgent matters first) sometimes represses in Sade is, precisely, his writing. Yet, what else would be repressed? Sade's writing is the 'purloined letter'.

It seems to me that it is at this point in the necessary work accomplished by that criticism in the last twenty or so years that your intervention comes. You, who belong to another generation, separate Sade a little from our temptations (perhaps also because we have had the merit to write of them). Without taking any of his radicalism from him, you in some small measure smooth out the extremes we gave him. Thus, as your chapters unfold, you are able to allow us to divine the true force of Sade which is—even if this terminology is not yours—the writing of fantasy, which we can also pass through the mirror and term the fantasy of writing. Sade isn't a writer like the others and yet he is a writer—perhaps *the* writer—since he is shackled by no law (either philosophical or political, as you show), except precisely the very secret and very manifest law (the purloined letter again!) of the Sentence. What Sentences Sade writes! Building upon Foucault's expression, you offer a very good analysis of the Sadean 'lightning'. I would happily add to that chapter something that would not, I think, run counter to it—namely, that Sade's lightning (the bolt that descends on us almost two centuries later and runs through us from mouth to sex) is that of writing.

One last word. I would like to see your book, which is short, as an argument. *Argumentum* is that which is sharp, clear, brilliant (like silver—the root is the same), but it is also that which summarizes as it articulates. It remains, then, for you to 'de-summarize' all that, to delve deep into the case you have so brilliantly outlined for us. I read your book more or less as a 'prospectus' (a word used by another Sadean, Fourier) for a forthcoming study of Sade that you have within you: Sade 'as his writing makes him'.

Preface
(Encyclopédie Bordas, Volume IX:
L'Aventure littéraire de l'humanité II)

*Oeuvres
complètes,*
Volume 4,
pp. 980–2

In all the literatures of the world, which are almost as numerous as its languages, we find a common feature—literature is almost always and everywhere *a language apart*. This excluded language, which is both granted higher status and, at the same time, closely monitored, is clearly a practice of signification that *exceeds* the mere communicative purpose science ordinarily assigns to language.

There is, then, a global identity of literature, which relates to the constancy of its situation amid the other forms of language. We should, however, be under no illusions: only at a very elevated, very formal level is literature a universal fact. But for us as Westerners, raised with a sense of our civilization's superiority, and for us as enquirers into knowledge and encyclopaedia-readers, what matters isn't the unity of literature but something we are poorly prepared for and poorly informed about—namely, the strangely neglected *dispersion* of the literary phenomenon. We have to learn that there are—ad infinitum—*other literatures*: this purely common-sense rule isn't easy to apply, since we are reluctant to imagine discourses we neither own nor stand at the centre of. It's a *journey* we have to go on, then (I'm almost tempted to use the word *trip* but in the sense that word has in drug parlance); we have to set about the salutary learning of a distance. Let us list the stages here, the successively wider circles, since this is a book that gradually carries us into more and more exotic territory.

The starting point is our own literature, not at all out of a sense of nationality but because literature is the glorious essence of the mother tongue. Our literature is our mother; we are attached to it as to a centre, an origin, a basic form of sustenance, a reassurance. Within it, all seems familiar, familial; outside it, everything begins to seem strange.

The circle beyond this isn't far removed from our own; a merely regional distance is involved. The English, German, Italian and Spanish literatures hardly take us away from home, perhaps because they are products, more or less, of the same history as our own. Travelling through these adjoining literatures has scarcely any more effect than a trip to London, Munich or Florence. We find the same churches, the same museums, the same poems. There are just a few tiny disparities in local custom: in one place they drink beer and not wine, in another they produce terza rima, not alexandrines. Goldoni is, admittedly, different from Molière, but hardly any more different than Jean-François Regnard.

The true Other begins a little further away, at the point where the very 'soul' of the literary population (authors and characters) seems put together in unfamiliar proportions and with unusual emphases. This second distance is, for example, that of Russian literature (which we have only very recently come to know).

The third distance might be said to be metaphysical in kind—it is the distance imposed on us by literatures such as the Chinese or the Japanese. With these, we know only that they are of major significance. In this case, the alien nature of the names and customs and the peculiarity of the characters are not the only elements in the representation that are strange. Beyond superficial questions of custom, there remains a deep divide with regard to the human subject, which is not, in those countries, the product of the same metaphysical, theological and psychological forces that lend the Western self its 'natural' consistency.

However, one last distance is possible (this is our fourth circle)—the distance that separates us from the literatures we might call ethnographic, by dint of their emergence in minor areas of our planet (such as the Tamil, Bengali, Dalmatian literatures, etc.). For us, as Westerners, as a result of the most powerful censorship, these literatures are not even regarded as having value or, in other words, as being part of culture.

This brief journey tells us that in a work of scholarship such as this, what is at issue is to let the Other speak, to give the Other a right to language. Now, it is, admittedly, not yet texts but lists of names that are granted this right here. Yet naming is the ritual act that determines knowledge; as soon as we know that a Coptic, Finnish or Sanskrit literature exists, or has existed, we can sense there will be genres, periods, authors. We feel a desire to go further into the foreign text, the text foreign to our ways. And then we better understand what a *distance* is—it is a space given to us by history not so that we may abolish or overcome it but so that we may make it, just as it is, a part of our truth. That truth which is ours because, being buried in our Unconscious, we are not acquainted with it.

Interview–Preface

(Littérature occidentale)

This 'preface in the form of an interview' was used by the publishing houses Grammont and Laffont to introduce the 85th book in their series 'La Bibliothèque Laffont des grands thèmes', entitled *La Littérature Occidentale* (Western Literature). The work is subtitled 'Birth and Development of Literature in the West. The Evolution of Modern Literary Genres' and was published in 1976.

Oeuvres complètes, Volume 4, pp. 985–91

In what way is 'literature' differentiated from other modes of written expression?

First of all, we need to take into account here that the question 'What is literature?' arose only relatively recently. In our Western culture, literature was being produced for a very long time before anyone really advanced a theory of literature, a theory of what literature *is*. This was particularly the case in France. Whereas the nineteenth century was a great century of scientific progress in the human and social sciences, unfortunately we stood out, if I may put it that way, by our theoretical shortcomings in respect of literature. There was, admittedly, an entire movement engaged in the analysis of literary works but no one really raised the problem of a philosophy of literature or, even less, of a scientific criticism. In France, we don't have the equivalent of a major philosophical, historical synthesis such as was produced by Hegel in Germany with regard to the various types of art. So a question of this kind is relatively recent. It arises today in a very acute theoretical form, particularly in avant-garde works and texts. And it's about relating the phenomenon of literature to the major new disciplines of the human sciences, such as political critique or psychoanalysis. It is, in fact, only since this scientific environment has existed that people have begun to ask: 'What is literature?'

What is the relationship between literature and other artistic modes of expression? Is it, itself, a form of artistic expression?

If we agree, provisionally, to respond in a traditional manner, we might say that literary expression is indisputably a phenomenon of an aesthetic type, with the same status as painting, sculpture, music or, now, cinema. However, literature is a form of artistic expression that operates by way of very precise signs—the signs of writing. This is an important point. Literature is essentially a written phenomenon. Even though many countries have an oral literature, for us Westerners, literature is above all a written object.

In literature there seems to be an ambiguity between form and content, which isn't the case in music, for example . . .

That ambiguity exists insofar as literature is made up of a quantity of *messages* (as we say today)—of very particular utterances. The message conveys ideas, feelings or passions, as we used to put it, but at the same time it has a very determinate form, which is of an aesthetic kind ...

Without form, no literature! And, indeed, copyright protects only form ...

The form is genuinely the idiolectal mark, the author's individual mark on the work.

'The style is the man,' as they say. Are we now in a position to give a much more precise definition of what style is?

Attempts to establish a science of style—that is to say, a stylistics, a way of scientifically studying authors' styles—have been going on for fifty years or more. We have to admit that as yet these attempts have largely failed. There are, in fact, many schools of stylistics, but none is very convincing. It's a science that's still in the making. Style is an undeniable reality, but it appears to be extremely difficult to define the phenomenon objectively, in terms of scientific criteria.

One of the latest—serious, intelligent and interesting—attempts to produce a stylistics is the work that's developed around an American scholar of French origins, [Michel] Riffaterre. It's a stylistics that postulates the existence of a kind of normal language—for example, the French language—a common usage that would serve, as it were, as model or standard. The thing then would be to assess the ways each author departed from this model. As Riffaterre sees it, stylistics is defined as the science of discrepancies, and it's on this basis that his position is hotly contested now, for reasons that are both philosophical and scientific. According a pre-eminent function to the way the majority of people use the language isn't regarded as an adequate scientific criterion.

How have the literary genres, as symbolized by the nine muses of Greek mythology, evolved?

I could tell you—without, for all that, being content with such a superficially plausible answer—that in the last 2,500 years, since the Greeks, the different literary genres have known spells of fashionability, decline, recovery, etc., but, throughout, there have always been literary genres. This means that, right up to our own day, literature has always been divided up according to a very precise code. That code ranged lyric poetry, idylls, dramatic poetry and epics against one another, for example; it also ranged verse against prose, the novel against the essay, the short story against the folk tale, etc.

So literature has always fallen under the strictures of an extremely precise, extremely constraining general code, even if that code has changed its content in different periods. Yet now—and this is why your question has very topical significance—in the work being done by the avant-garde, there's a most lively, most persistent and quite rigorous attempt to subvert the very idea of literary genre. In fact, the view is today that there are ultimately no watertight barriers between the different types of written production. We can now conceive of producing something that will simply be called a *text*. This is the word that's used now, rather than literary 'work'. The text may be seen at the same time as both a novel and an essay.

The walls that once stood between the different genres are falling away now. That had already been the case in a few rare works in the past, but artistic exploration is now moving generally in that direction.

Can we say that literature is also a social language? What relationship is there between literature and society?

Literature is steeped in sociality. Its materials come essentially from society, from the history of society. It's inconceivable that we could write even the slightest text without history getting into it in some way—and society with its divisions, conflicts and problems, of course. But you always have that mediation of form, which means the literary work is never a pure and simple reflection of society. There are reverberation effects, the transposition isn't direct. It's very difficult to analyse a literary work purely in terms of reflection. That's never quite how it is. But at the same time, history is always there. It's the study of this space of ambiguity, of the presence/absence of society in literature that constitutes the privileged field of literary activity.

Between a Dadaist manifesto, a poem produced by the Surrealist 'automatic writing' technique, a Soviet novel following the conventions of Socialist realism and certain very dense texts by the new wave of writers, there's a whole world of difference . . .

Yes, the modes of presence of society in literary works spread across a very wide spectrum. But there's another aspect to this too: literary works are consumed very unequally by different social groups . . .

Literature is also a means of communication of social facts . . .

It's always a reflection on society—often a critical reflection.

The social effectiveness of literature and the influence works have on the public aren't necessarily related to the level of their sales. Don't some authors, today, have an influence quite disproportionate to their actual readerships?

You're referring to a recent sociological phenomenon there. There's a relatively common discrepancy these days between, let's say, an author's notoriety and the print runs of his books. You currently have writers whose books are printed in very small numbers but who have considerable intellectual notoriety. By contrast, some authors who sell huge numbers of books aren't known at all. This kind of discrepancy or divorce between the two is a phenomenon that's generally on the increase, because the audience for literature is no longer confined to the upper middle classes or, where mass-market literature is concerned, to certain popular strata. There's now a mediating milieu in which the notoriety of a work or a writer spreads and this enlarges the waves of notoriety, so to speak. Roughly speaking, that milieu is formed by the intellectuals. In the past, in order to become known, a book was necessarily subjected to—and passed through—a form of organized criticism. I wonder whether that criticism still plays a very important role these days. What's decisive, on the other hand, is a sort of intellectual rumour mill that substantially increases the impact of literary works.

What, in your opinion, is the role of literature in contemporary thought?

Before the last war it would have been quite easy to answer your question, simply by highlighting the extreme importance of great writers. I'm thinking here of France that had a kind of leadership in the world of culture. People like Gide, Valéry, Montherlant, Malraux and so on had absolutely key positions in the cultural world.

What do we find now? There's no leadership any more and no great writers with this kind of sacred role vested in them. The last such person, we might venture, was Sartre. But Sartre himself is engaged in a kind of thinking that aims precisely to destroy the authority of the writer . . .

Literature in itself—that is to say, in its traditional form—occupies less and less of a place in culture and thought. By contrast, philosophy, for example—the social body of philosophers—is increasingly interested in literature. There's a kind of coming-together and overlapping of genres going on here . . .

What's the function of literary criticism today?

There are (or were not so long ago) two types of criticism—one that I'd call 'launch' criticism, which takes a book on its publication and contributes to propelling it into the public sphere through daily or weekly coverage of literature in standard media outlets (news-papers, magazines, radio stations or TV channels) and another, existing alongside it, that I'd call 'structural criticism', which isn't concerned first and foremost with topical literary events but is trying to rethink the instrument of criticism—that is to say, to interrogate the very idea of literature.

I have the impression that this structural criticism is a little less robust than it was five years ago. The last twenty years have been a great time for this form of work, either in the form of thematic analyses (with Bachelard, Jean-Pierre Richard and Starobinski), or a more structuralist, semiological, linguistic criticism (particularly with Gérard Genette).

How do you see relations developing between the audio-visual media and literature?

Personally, I have a highly subjective view of this question, dominated by the most extreme analytic caution. It's a commonplace to say we're leaving the age of

Pisces and will soon be entering the age of Aquarius—that we are changing sign. It may be that we are leaving the era of writing to enter that of the image. Having belonged to a writing-based civilization, it might be said we're beginning to be part of an image-based one . . .

For my part, I believe the problem is much more complex. What may happen is the development of new relations between the image and writing. But writing will always have a crucial function in society, unless there is some great historical cataclysm of a political kind (which is always possible).

There will be complementary roles for the two. However, writing should retain a function that we have to understand in all its subtlety and, indeed, almost its paradoxicality. Writing doesn't simply have the function of communicating or disseminating things widely, it also perhaps has the function of keeping them secret to some extent, of concealing them. If we look closely at the history of writing, we see that it has had two roles. One the one hand, it served to communicate. But it also served to keep a sort of silence around some things, a kind of secrecy or, at least, to limit access to them. It may very well be that society today has need of a slightly more difficult area of thought or communication. None of this means that books are to lose their function.

Let's come back a little to sociology. As soon as you accept that there's a code that's perceptible only to a certain elite, to certain technocrats, you favour a sort of reserved domain, you establish a real process of selection . . .

The way I see it, the problem is precisely to change the social nature of the elite that might profit from that kind of closed space. Projecting things forward in a utopian way, we might very well imagine certain writings being circulated in a rather clandestine way, but a way that isn't at all linked or limited to a social group in power. I'm absolutely not talking about an elitism. I believe that we don't currently have a sufficient grasp of this problem of the image and writing. Attempts have been made, such as those of McLuhan for example. It's all very exciting, but difficult to analyse. We're very much in a time of change.

Literature is becoming international and raises problems of translation . . .

The difficulties arise from the fact that literary practice deeply involves language. But what literary practice involves is one's maternal language, one's mother tongue. There's a relationship between the writer and his mother tongue, which means that translations are absolutely indispensable but ultimately always inadequate.

If a text is truly literary, it involves a relation between the writer's body and his mother tongue which cannot come through in translation. When we read literary works in translation, we're communicating with a certain universe, but it isn't the essential universe of the work which is, in other words, its language.

If we look at the statistics today, we see that the proportion of published material that is literature seems to be on the decrease. How do you view the future of literature and its development?

This is a question that has far too many factors to it—political factors, factors of income levels, education and knowledge, and planetary factors too, insofar as history has become global. It's very difficult to come to a view. I think literature will always be driven to forge wildly ahead of the rest of society. It will always have an ambiguous role of expressing society's discontents or troubles, so long as those exist, but also a utopian role, a role of representing certain utopias. While ever the world is historically alienated, literature will have this dual function.

From Them
to Us

This article, first published in *Le Monde* of 7 April 1978, appeared in a section entitled 'Voltaire and Rousseau'.

    On the copy of the article preserved in his own archives, Barthes made a handwritten note to the effect that it had been abridged by the newspaper. It is the full text which is published here.

Oeuvres complètes, Volume 5, pp. 454–5

Voltaire-and-Rousseau—there they are, then, the pair of them, true to their appointed roles in our literary history and national mythology. They are a couple as inseparable as Bouvard and Pécuchet, Rolls and Royce or Romeo and Juliet, and their status as contrasting, yet complementary, twins satisfies the demands of the old Romantic myth of 'the head and the heart'.[1] Sufficient cause, perhaps, not to bother to read them any more. And yet, by chance as I was working on something else, I leafed through a few pages of Voltaire and Rousseau recently. And the miracle happened (I call it a miracle when a pleasure one was looking forward to does, despite the circumstances, occur): I smiled at Voltaire and dreamt of Rousseau.

---

1 In the original, Barthes refers not to Rolls and Royce but to the lift manufacturers Roux and Combaluzier who were, long ago, a byword in French for this sort of inseparable partnership. [Trans.]

From the 'Dialogue between the Cock and the Hen', here is Voltaire: 'COCK: Good lord, my dear hen, you do look sad: what's wrong? HEN: Dear friend, better ask what's *not* wrong with me. An awful servant took me on her knees, stuck a long needle up my backside, grabbed hold of my womb, rolled it around the needle, tore it out and gave it to her cat to eat . . .'[2] Where, in heaven's name, is this story of animal hysterectomy leading? Only gradually will I come to see, prodded on by my curiosity yet kept in suspense by the storyteller's art, that the aim is to heap opprobrium on castrati, the Church, emperors and kings, the pyres of the Inquisition, priests, Christians, religious hypocrisy and intolerance, while nodding approvingly along the way to 'good' civilizations, paganism and India. Voltaire sets out from the trivial and maintains that trivial air with the sheer drive of his narrative, but along the way sweeps up every subject of any seriousness whatever: history, ideas, civilizations, crimes, ritual, bad faith—in short, all the clamorous issues of the world we are still wrestling with today. Which brings us to the modern question: Why (as I see it, at least) is there no art of intellectual persuasion or imagination today? Why are we so ponderous, so unconcerned to mobilize story and image? Can we not see that it is, after all, works of fiction—however mediocre they may

2 Voltaire, 'Dialogue between the Cock and the Hen' (Haydn and Adrienne Mason trans.) *Comparative Criticism* 20 (1998): 184. [Trans.]

be artistically (one thinks of Solzhenitsyn)—that best stir political feeling? Now, don't just say, 'Well, all right, do it yourself!' Perhaps we believe in fewer things than Voltaire. Perhaps we feel more *hopeless* than the wry-faced—though tender-eyed (Michelet)—philosopher of old.

Rousseau writes (and this is better known): 'Night was falling. I saw the sky, a few stars, and a little greenery. This first sensation was a moment of delight. It alone gave me some feeling of myself. In that instant I was born into life, and it seemed to me as if I was filling all the things I saw with my frail existence' (from 'The Second Walk').[3] There, in a word, on an October evening in 1776, we have the subject 'deconstructed' (as we would say now). The ego is there, admittedly, but only the better to express that it is absent from itself, expelled from full consciousness, at the outer limits of itself, at the point where it dissolves into the *moment*. It is the moment that is subjective and individual, not the subject or the individual. This is a theme that is still so obscure (it has a promising future before it) that we see Deleuze working courageously on it today. More than this, classicism drags Rousseau's notation into a sort of 'super-avant-garde' and allows us to hear the music of something that lies, as yet,

---

3 Jean-Jacques Rousseau, *The Reveries of the Solitary Walker* (Russell Goulbourne trans.) (Oxford: Oxford University Press, 2011). [Trans.]

ROLAND BARTHES

beyond our ken: the abandonment of all paroxysm, the relinquishment of that violence of language which we believe to be 'modern' but which is simply the repression of a value that is, nonetheless, well known in other civilizations (I am thinking of the Orient)—*minimal existence*. For 'existing' isn't something we necessarily experience in violence but something also felt in these '*few* stars', this '*little* greenery'—these sparse things that gave Rousseau his 'point of departure' or, in other words, enabled him to tell his story. For here we are again with Narrative and here again with the modern question that faces us—or the constraint we are reminded of: How are we to write without ego? It is my hand that makes the traces, not my neighbour's. In order to say I am dispensing with the classical subject, wanting nothing to do with it any more and regarding it, indeed, as impossible, I have to hold on to it for one moment more, the moment it takes to write a sentence.

A Voltaire less hopeless and a Rousseau happier than we are? Perhaps it is because they didn't know (and no one around them knew) that *language exists*, that we have to bear it, work on it, enjoy it as though it were our very body, the contradictory condition of our alienation and our liberation, of our ponderousness and our lightness.

'It All Comes Together'

Oeuvres complètes, Volume 5, pp. 654–6

In 1979, Barthes was teaching a course at the Collège de France entitled 'La Préparation du roman', lectures translated into English as *The Preparation of the Novel* (New York: Columbia University Press, 2011). One of his aims in that course was to explore the relationship between teaching and literary creation and the ways in which the one might stimulate the other. This article, published in *Le Magazine littéraire* of January 1979, a mass-market magazine easily available from French newsstands, is perhaps best read in that context.

I have retained the French title of Proust's masterpiece *A la recherche du temps perdu*. On the question of English translations, see p. 70.

There are, it seems, few enigmas in literary history. Yet here is one that has Proust as its hero. It intrigues and interests me, particularly as it is an *enigma relating to creation* (the only sort of relevance to someone who wants to write).

People are fond of repeating that Proust wrote only one work, *A la recherche du temps perdu*, and that, even if that work is nominally a late one, all the minor publications that preceded were merely foreshadowings. That may well be. Proust's creative life has, nonetheless, two very distinct parts to it. Until 1909, Proust lived the high-society life. He wrote this and that and was published now and again, but despite his efforts and explorations his great work didn't 'come together'. The death of his mother in 1905 was a great shock to him and it led to his withdrawal for a time from society, but the desire to write soon returned, without his being able to overcome a certain sterile agitation. However, agitation gradually focused itself down into the form of indecision: Was he going to (did he want to) write a novel or a work of non-fiction? He attempted non-fiction with an essay contesting the ideas of Sainte-Beuve,[1] though the style was novelistic, since, mixed in with fragments on literary aesthetics were set-pieces, scenes, dialogues and characters that would later appear in *A la recherche*. This set of essays (I am straining the word) called *Contre Sainte-Beuve* forms a manuscript which he submitted to *Le Figaro* in July 1909 and was rejected in the August.[2] At this point there is a puzzling episode about which we know nothing, a 'silence' that constitutes the enigma I spoke of. What is happening in that month of September 1909 in the life or the mind of Proust? The fact is that his biography shows him, by the October of that year, already pitching himself into the great work to which he will, henceforth, sacrifice everything, withdrawing from the world in order to write it and just managing to complete it before he is thwarted by death. So there are two parts to Proust's life, two contrasting aspects that come either side of September 1909: before that point, worldliness and creative hesitancy; after it, withdrawal and firmness of intention (obviously, I am simplifying).

[1] Charles Augustin Sainte-Beuve (1804–69) was one of the most prominent French literary critics of the nineteenth century. He favoured a strong biographical element in the critical approach to literature. [Trans.]

[2] See Marcel Proust, *Against Sainte-Beuve and Other Essays* (John Sturrock trans.) (London: Penguin, 1994). [Trans.]

What is at play in this change is, as I see it, the following: all Proust's writings preceding *A la recherche* are, to some degree, fragmentary and short—short stories, articles, scraps of texts. One has the impression that the ingredients are present (as we say in cooking), but the operation that's going to transform them into a dish hasn't yet taken place: it's 'not quite there'. And then, suddenly (in September 1909), 'it all comes together': the mayonnaise thickens and it's just a question of gradually producing more and more. Moreover, Proust increasingly works with a technique of 'adding-in'—he is constantly re-infusing food into this organism which now begins to thrive because it is well set up. The physical writing itself changes: admittedly, Proust always wrote 'at the gallop', as he put it (and that manual rhythm is perhaps not unrelated to the movement of his sentences), but at the point when *A la recherche* takes off, the writing changes—it 'tightens', 'becomes more complex' and overflows now with energetic emendations. To sum up: a kind of alchemical operation occurred within Proust during that month of September which transmuted the essay into a novel and a short, discontinuous thing into a long, sustained, fully formed one.

What happened? Why was it that all of a sudden, in a summer month, 'it all came together' and remained so for ever (until Proust's death in 1922 and far beyond, since our present, active reading is constantly adding to *A la recherche*, feeding it up)? I don't believe in any determining factor from the biographical sphere.

Private events may, admittedly, have a decisive effect on literary work, but that influence is complex and operates with a time delay. There is no doubt that the death of his mother was, in some sense, a 'founding moment' of *A la recherche*, but the book was not begun until four years after her death. I believe, rather, in some discovery of a creative order: Proust found a way—perhaps a purely technical way—to make the work 'hold together' and to 'facilitate' his writing (in the operational sense).

Intuitively, I shall argue that what was found probably belongs to one of the following 'techniques' (or to more than one at the same time):

(1) A certain way of saying 'I', an original mode of utterance that refers, undecidably, to the author, the narrator and the protagonist.

(2) A (poetic) 'truth' of the proper names that had finally been settled on. Proust hesitated for a long time over the main names in *A la recherche*. The book seems to take off when the 'correct' names are found, and we know that there is a theory of proper names in the novel itself.

(3) A change of scale: it may, in fact, happen (by some mysterious chemistry) that a project which has been stalled for a long time suddenly becomes possible once one suddenly—and in inspired fashion—decides to increase its size. For in the aesthetic order, the dimensions of a thing determine its meaning.

(4) Lastly, a novelistic structure which Proust discovers as a revelation in Balzac's *Comédie humaine*, and which is (I'm quoting Proust) 'Balzac's admirable invention of having kept the same characters in all his novels'—a procedure deprecated by Sainte-Beuve, but, in Proust's view, an idea of genius. When one knows the importance of recurrences, coincidences and reversals throughout *A la recherche* and how proud Proust was of his mode of composition by 'enjambment', whereby an insignificant detail given at the beginning of the novel reappears at the end, as though it had grown, germinated and blossomed, the thought arises that what Proust discovered was the effectiveness for novel-writing of what we might call the (horticultural) 'layering' of figures: a figure 'planted' at one point, often discreetly (let us take the example at random of the 'lady in pink'), reappears much later, having jumped across an infinity of other relationships, and becomes the root of a new growth within the novel (Odette).

All this should be researched more thoroughly, from both the biographical and structural standpoints. And for once, scholarship would perhaps be justified by the fact that it would be enlightening to 'those who wish to write'.

Masculine, Feminine, Neuter

Oeuvres complètes, Volume 5, pp. 1027–43

The following text, which appears in the 'Annexes' to Volume 5 of the latest French edition of Barthes's Complete Works, was written in 1967 but not published until three years later when it appeared in a *Festschrift* marking Claude Lévi-Strauss's 60th birthday: Jean Pouillon and Pierre Maranda (eds), *Échanges et communications. Mélanges offerts à Claude Lévi-Strauss* (The Hague: Mouton, 1970).

It was, in the words of Barthes's editor Éric Marty, the 'first outline' of *S/Z*, Barthes's more detailed structural analysis of the novella *Sarrasine*, which was also published in 1970 by Éditions du Seuil. Marty says that a note on the manuscript suggests that it was written in the summer of 1967 (see Roland Barthes, *Sarrasine de Balzac. Séminaires à l'École pratique des hautes études, 1967–68, 1968–69*. Paris: Seuil, 2011, p. 17).

Sarrasine is a short novella that Balzac ranged among his *Scenes of Parisian Life*. Here is a summary of that novella.

Attending a Parisian party, the narrator falls for a moment into a daydream, struck by the fantastic contrast between the garden of the grand house he is at—a garden lying deserted and dead beneath the snow—and the sparkling atmosphere of the salon. A conversation informs us that the fortune of the owners, the Lanty, comes of unknown origin. The Lanty family is made up of the father, a sad, ugly banker, the mother and two very handsome children, Marianina and Filippo. At one point a character appears, presumably a relative, given the attentiveness of the family: he is an enigmatic creature, an old man lavishly attired and made up, who produces a strange impression of coldness all around him. The Marquise de Rochefide, who is being courted by the narrator, feels a lively curiosity towards him and, at the same time, a strong sense of repulsion. Moving on to a boudoir, Mme de Rochefide discovers a wonderful painting depicting an Adonis 'too beautiful for a man'. The picture was painted from a statue of a woman. The model, says the narrator, was a member of Mme de Lanty's family. Who is the old man? Who is the Adonis? At Mme de Rochefide's insistence, the narrator promises to go to her home the next day and clear up the mystery. This he does.

Ernest-Jean Sarrasine, the son of a prosecutor from the Franche-Comté was raised by Jesuits. From childhood, his character was strange, violent, passionate and ungodly, 'both active and passive by turns'. Expelled from college, he entered the studio of the sculptor Bouchardon, who took him under his wing. The wild Sarrasine led a life of strenuous toil—sculpture was his only mistress. In 1758, he left for Italy. A few days after his arrival in Rome, he went to the Teatro Argentina where an opera by Jomelli was being staged. The appearance of the *prima donna* had a dramatic effect on Sarrasine—all the perfections of the female form seem to him to be united in la Zambinella, perfections which, in his experience as a sculptor, he has only ever known as fragments or details. Seized with a mad passion, he decides he will be loved by la Zambinella or die. Sarrasine then becomes an assiduous patron of the theatre, where his passion is known to the actors. One evening, la Zambinella casts a glance in his direction and, at the end of the performance and in spite of a warning Sarrasine receives—la Zambinella is protected by

Cardinal Cicognara—a duenna takes him to a supper party at the home of an actor. There he comes face to face with la Zambinella, who is both provocative and reserved, and whose extreme delicacy he finds both striking and charming, seeing in it the very essence of femininity. Although la Zambinella tries to dissuade Sarrasine from pursuing a passion she describes as impossible, the sculptor is undeterred and resolves to kidnap her. On the evening the abduction is due to take place, the sculptor attends a private party at which la Zambinella is to sing. The female singer appears dressed as a man. As Sarrasine seeks an explanation for this disguise, one of the guests informs the naive sculptor that in Italy women never appear on the stage—Zambinella is a castrato. Realizing that her lover is becoming aware of the truth and fearing the violence of his disappointment, Zambinella stops singing. Sarrasine leaves the party, apparently driven to distraction. Determined to know (since he still doubts whether Zambinella is not indeed a woman), he abducts the *musico* and locks her up in his studio. Terrorized, Zambinella confirms his true nature: he only went along with Sarrasine's passion for the sake of his friends, who wanted to make fun of the sculptor. In his madness and desperation, Sarrasine attempts to destroy the statue he had made of la Zambinella and hurls himself on the singer to kill him. At that point, three of Cardinal Cicognara's men enter and run Sarrasine through. As he expires, he welcomes his death as a blessing.

Mme de Rochefide asks the narrator what connection there can be between this story of the strange old man who made his appearance at the Lantys' gathering and the Adonis of the picture. The narrator then explains that the old man and the Adonis (painted by Vien from Sarrasine's statue) are none other than la Zambinella, the castrato once famed throughout Europe and possessor of a vast fortune that is enjoyed by his family, the Lantys, who are consequently concerned to conceal the origins of their wealth. Mme de Rochefide is pensive and muses on how life is generally a disappointing affair, but the narrator counters with the idea that at least castrati are not being created any more.

As we know, linguistics is mainly based on the analysis of assertive models: assertion represents the norm (for example, Peter hits Paul) and interrogation is the deviation from it (as is negation). One consequence of this postulate is a natural confusion, which we commonly see today, between the structure of the grammatical sentence (noun + verb) and the structure of the predicative matrix (subject + predicate). In interrogation, by contrast, predication is uncertain or, at least, the four-part grouping of *noun*, *subject*, *verb* and *predicate* is subverted: in 'Who ran off? It was John', the verb is the subject and the noun the predicate. We would only need to overturn the implicit normality of the assertive paradigm and develop as the primary form a linguistics of interrogation (and response)—a linguistics from which assertion would, in its turn, be merely the deviation, or for which it would serve as a disguise—for the recognized universals of language (noun-verb, subject-predicate) to become suspect. Now, a linguistics of questioning would be enormously useful in the structural analysis of narrative; in fact, assertion merely supplies the details of the narration, the small change of the big picture that sums up the whole story; and that picture is essentially interrogative: 'suspense', the general form of narration, is clearly related closely to questioning—to a vital question, the uncertain answer to which is particularly delayed.

Every narrative, it would seem, basically involves a question. Classical narratives—the narratives of Western literature—can, insofar as they are simple, be reduced to four main questions, four kinds of 'suspense'. Two of these forms are related to *being* and two to *doing*. In the first form of suspense, the narrative is concerned with deferring—and answering—the question *who*? (Who did that? Who, in reality, is this character? etc.). Among other narratives, the classic detective novel, in which the question relates to the identity of a murderer, is of this first type. In the second, rarer form of suspense, the question of identity relates not to the proper name of the unknown person but, if we may put it this way, to his species name, his common name: here 'who?' becomes 'what?' (What is it?). Some detective stories (e.g. *The Hound of the*

Baskervilles) and some science-fiction narratives develop this second form of suspense. The third type is the most banal and provides the model for all 'dramatic' narratives—here the question is about the outcome of the action: Will this end well or badly? Who will win out? Will Captain Grant's children find their father again? Will Lucien de Rubempré be saved? There are, lastly, narratives whose outcome the reader (or listener) knows from the outset, yet whose structure is manifestly suspensive: the question is then about the way the outcome is achieved: to this last type of suspense belong both tragedy, based on a mechanism of inevitability, and the recursive narrative, where the outcome is given first and only thereafter do we discover its source using the technique of flashbacks.

This is a rudimentary typology and we shall not linger over it: the point is simply to suggest that the four questions we have just identified are found in Balzac's *Sarrasine*, which is based like this on multiple and, as it were, total suspense. The first question of identity attaches to the enigmatic old man at the Lantys' party, where what is at stake is the discovery of his proper name (*Who* is he?) or, in other words, his social, parental, historical status, his place in the world, his relationship to the Lanty family, his origin. The second question (*What?*) is what gives the novella its special character. Here again, the question relates to the old man and, even more, to la Zambinella: What is their nature? The question does not, properly speaking, revolve around a choice of names but around the very possibility of naming: what is suggested, interrogatively, is rather the category of the unnameable, of the *thing* in the fantastical sense of the term. The suspense with regard to being is not a matter of ignorance here but an enigma. The old man is terrifying after the fashion of something unnameable (he gives off a coldness, he cannot be touched) and Sarrasine dies as soon as he can give la Zambinella his real name—it is the most terrible of all things because it is the *nothing* ('*You are nothing. If you were a man or a woman, I would kill you, but . . .*' [252]).[1] This suspense around the question of kind or species does not, however, constitute the entire interest of the novella. Even if we were to guess from the very beginning what the old man and la Zambinella are (in many people's reading, this must happen), the question remains—a drama now, not an enigma—'How is this going to end?'; the suspense with regard to *being* triggers, as it were, a suspense with regard to *doing*. The whole of the second part of the novella arises out of the way the drama (the story), which isn't hermeneutic in character, 'rubs against' the discourse, which is a decipherment whose trajectory is superimposed on the purely

[1] Since many English-speaking readers will have come to Balzac's *Sarrasine* through Barthes's *S/Z*, I have generally followed the English version of the novella which appears in Richard Miller's translation of that essay (New York: Farrar, Straus and Giroux, 1974), pp. 221–54. The page numbers in the text refer to that translation.

passional anxieties of Sarrasine. Lastly, the fourth form of suspense is hinted at; since the structure of the novella is a flashback (with its story within a story), a certain version of the outcome is given from the outset; if, for contingent reasons, we know from the beginning not only who the old man and la Zambinella are but also that Sarrasine is to die, it remains to gather together the pieces of the puzzle whose solution we already have and to complete the journey of its decipherment; or, more exactly, it remains for us to transfer on to the protagonist the ignorance that we need in order to have a good reading experience, to be watchers at the spectacle of *his* ignorance and to watch the way the truth that is known to us seeps into his awareness. This is a pattern that Brecht will use as the very mainspring of his theatre, presenting the spectator with the text of a blindness. That blindness is never dissipated since, in Brecht, the critical function is reserved for the audience not for the character, who is never a 'hero'. Yet, all in all, it isn't clear either that Sarrasine, discovering the true nature of la Zambinella, really knows his own truth for all that.

The (multi-layered) process of decipherment that underlies Balzac's novella cannot be conceived as a unilateral operation: in no sense is the text enciphered by the author then deciphered by the reader. The signs offering themselves for decipherment are, at the same moment, the signs of encipherment: the reader deciphers and enciphers at the same time—he perceives what is written as both an obscure and a clear cipher. This ambiguity is further supported by the fact that in *Sarrasine* the reader is never directly the one doing the deciphering—the novella includes its own internal processes of decipherment. There are two of these: one such process has the prologue as its stage, the enigmatic old man as its object and Mme de Rochefide as its subject (that subject being led by the words of the narrator); the other has as its stage the reported anecdote, its object is la Zambinella and its subject the sculptor Sarrasine. The unity of the two decipherings is achieved only at the level of their objects: in substantial terms, because in each case it is a body that is deciphered; in civil terms, because in both cases it is the same body that is deciphered; in structural terms, because the two ciphers, which are separated at first, converge in the epilogue, where their objects coincide ('But this Zambinella—he or she?' 'He, madame, is none other than Marianina's great uncle.' [253]). And yet, that common object does not offer itself up to the reader in the same way: in the case of the old man, the problem faced by the decipherer is one of gathering together a fragmented identity, of conjuring up a unitary name that does not yet exist, since, where the strange old man is concerned, neither the person nor the body can be named. Zambinella, by contrast, possesses a clear, assembled, named identity (she is a singer); by contrast with the first case, the problem here is to undermine that identity, to unmask a body, to substitute one noun (castrato) for another (woman), one substance (the *nothing*) for another (full, perfect femininity).

Hence the tactics of decipherment are not the same in the two series. In the first, out of the absence of a name a name has to be made; in the manner of an analysis into component parts carried out in reverse, the encipherment consists in this case in disseminating a number of 'semes' throughout the prologue, semes which, when—later—added together, are to form the signified 'old castrato'. The 'creature' will, as a result be provided with (i) old age; (ii) femininity; (iii) infantility; (iv) wealth (famous castrati amassed fabulous fortunes); (v) musicality (the old man trembles nostalgically at the trill executed by his great-niece); (vi) a last characteristic that is difficult to name since what is at issue is precisely that 'nothing' which makes the castrato: Balzac presents this through the theme of the mannequin (a creature resplendent in make-up, decked out in a curly blond wig)—that is to say, the theme of the inanimate *thing* (alluded to in the repellent coldness the enigmatic creature gives off). All these 'semes' are spread throughout the fabric of the narrative, coming together under the name of la Zambinella only at the last minute. This Zambinella, for her part, cannot be comprised of 'semes', or, at least, if she is made up of them, they can only ever be semes of femininity: Sarrasine *reads* Zambinella as a woman and nothing in the anecdote ever 'semantically' belies 'her' femininity; in la Zambinella castration is revealed by confession, not by decipherment.

What Sarrasine actually rejects in la Zambinella, in fury and dread, is an idea, not a reality; the castrato becomes an object of decipherment only when he is grown old, when he has passed from the status of illusion to that of thing. In this way, meaning appears as the belated truth of the illusion but illusion itself is outside of meaning; it does not lend itself, in any way, to an objective hermeneutics. In terms of the level of description, which is supreme, the 'reality' is that la Zambinella is a woman; the illusion is the *nothing* she confesses to. Balzac masterfully respected the subtle inversion in play here, all suggestions of the 'truth' (the castrato) being contradicted immediately by the clear evidence of 'reality' (the woman): '"And if I were not a woman?" la Zambinella asked in a soft, silvery voice' [247]. The two decipherments are based, admittedly, on an act of naming, but in the case of the old man, the name one is to be led to is, so to speak, lexical; it is the name of the thing in itself: it is a question of going back from the semes to the signified; in the case of la Zambinella, the name has definitional power only if it is proffered ('If I were to say one word, you would repulse me with horror.'): it is and remains a signifier, and its materiality (not its reference) will be the source of all Sarrasine's misfortune: and indeed, he doesn't dare pronounce it ('"Ah, you are a woman, the artist cried in a delirium, "for even a . . . " He broke off' [251]).

In Western literature of the realist type, the symbolic (by which I mean, generally, all substitutive discourse) is rationalized with psychological and historical justifications, which form the verisimilar layer of the story: the 'verisimilar' is what claims to escape the symbolic by deriving from an enthymematic (and syllogistic) model, not a metaphorical one. *Sarrasine* does not escape this constraint: it has three types of 'verisimilitude': the narrative, the psychological and the historic.

Narrative verisimilitude derives here from a very well-known model, that of the reported story or story within a story: the narrator is inside the story (since he is courting Mme de Rochefide) and outside it (for he is reporting it). The reported story derives increased verisimilitude from the fact that it eliminates—or seems to eliminate—the artifice of a purely cultural contact between an 'author' and a 'reader', entities that bear too greatly the mark of the literary institution. It seems, in fact, that the impersonal assertive mode (such as we find in both the indicative mood and the third-person novel) is not without its problems here and there: some languages, as we know, have a special mood intended to point up the contingent character of what is attested (the *testimonial* mood) and the novel, as we see, is very often tempted by these narratives of narratives, uttered more or less in the testimonial mood, which have the advantage of distancing by one notch the artifice of anonymous printed narration, thus restoring the—apparently rather nostalgic— memory of an oral literature: the story imitates history, writing imitates the spoken word, which is truer than it is itself, as though the mouth were a more natural organ than the hand.

Sarrasine also has a psychological verisimilitude. That verisimilitude is constituted by a romantic stereotype: the battle of the artist—presented as an invincible individual, with his absolute passion and solitary suffering—against society, presented as a thing of censorship, closure and incomprehension. Since verisimilitude plays a role of furnishing reasons, this cliché enables Sarrasine's adventure to be *explained*: the sculptor is an artist absorbed in his dreams and passions, a kind of ill-adapted savage, an unpractical man who sees nothing outside his own fantasies and is unaware that in Italy women's roles are sung by castrati. La Zambinella, for her part, seems for a moment to share Sarrasine's passion (she grants him a kiss), but she is merely yielding, out of cowardice, to the desires of the derisive little group of actors who want to enjoy some fun at the Frenchman's expense by involving him in a ridiculous venture. Thus, the novella may pass for an allegory of the romantic solitude of the creative artist.

There is, lastly, in *Sarrasine*, a historical verisimilitude. Castrati, it should be remembered, did have a substantial place in seventeenth- and eighteenth-century Europe. That place wasn't without a certain mythic resonance: a Neapolitan castrato Farinelli, who had settled in Spain (and who died in 1782 at the age of 78), cured the melancholy of Philip V with his singing and the monarch never allowed him to leave again. The last two castrati had died, one in 1846, the other in 1861. Zambinella is almost their contemporary, since the prologue is set around 1830. At that point, Zambinella is some 90 years old. As the aged witness to a bygone society, he becomes the allegory of the radical break between the old society and the new: it is in this respect that *Sarrasine* is a scene from Parisian life.[2] The history of the castrato *explains* the inexplicable origins of the Parisian banker's fortune, an origin that is, in its way, fabulous, as is fitting in an age when there are no rules—and no hereditary dimension—to the acquisition of wealth. It is, indeed, at this point that symbols come into their own and verisimilitude is articulated as metaphor: the dimension of verisimilitude says that in the financial society of the Restoration, gold, the product of speculation and improper transfers of ownership, has, so to speak, no origin; metaphor says that this social vacuum has its counterpart in the lack that defines the castrato: to locate the origin of a fortune in the *nothing* of the castrato is, on the one hand, to limn out a perfectly verisimilar sociological process (the dates back it up) and, on the other, to assert the mythic subtlety of gold,

2 'Scenes from Parisian Life' was one of the sub-categories into which Balzac divided his *Comédie humaine* series, which consisted of more than 90 novels, stories and essays. The earliest works were (retrospectively) entitled 'Scenes from Private Life' and these were followed by 'Scenes from Provinicial Life', 'Scenes from Political Life', etc. [Trans.]

ROLAND BARTHES

the miraculous inflation of the zero (a theme we find again in Balzac's Mercadet, a financial schemer who makes gold out of nothing).

The argument here is not that verisimilitude occupies a superficial and fallacious role in the narrative. It is that symbols are inevitable and, even in the most sociological of our novelists, the explanatory project is full of metaphorical spaces. We must, then, turn to the symbolics of *Sarrasine*. Its apparent centre is sex. Clothing, a matter beloved of novelists, knows only two of these: male and female. Balzac, however, constantly has need of a third sex or an absence of sex. All that remains to him, then, is to define the state of castration either as a simultaneous mix of male and female (the old man's attire) or as the succession of the two (Zambinella dresses as a woman, then as a man). This vestimentary distribution well expresses the difficulty the novelist has in placing the castrato symbolically within the institutional structure of the sexes, which is ineluctably binary; for, if we confine ourselves to that structure, then since the unmarked item is the feminine one, what could the neuter consist in? In reality—and linguistics attests to this—the neuter cannot be directly part of a sexual structure; in European languages, the opposition between masculine and feminine is less important than that between animate and inanimate. And, indeed, it occurs subsequent to it:

Animate (Masculine/Feminine)/Inanimate (Neuter)

The major opposition between the animate and the neuter is marked morphologically in the very structure of the noun: the opposition between masculine and feminine appears only at the subsidiary level of the attribute (the adjective).[3] *Sarrasine* follows the guidance from linguistics—to the effect that the feminine is merely a substitute for the animate—very exactly here, since the masculine theme barely appears at all (except at the level of clothing): Zambinella isn't a cross-dressing male, she is something inanimate disguised as something animate. This is not the ambiguity of the invert but of the thing. The whole novella has just one paradigm, which isn't directly the paradigm of sex but that of life. Sarrasine doesn't depict a transgression of the categories of sex (like Séraphitüs/ Séraphita) but, if we may put it this way, a transgression of the categories of object, analogous to the transgression committed by most languages when they create metaphors: it is, in fact, the dual category of the *animate/inanimate* that is commonly subjected to metaphorical transgressions, not that of the *masculine/feminine* at all. Life or death? Such, here, is the site of the metaphor.[4]

3 A. Meillet, *Linguistique historique et Linguistique générale* (Paris: Édouard Champion, 1948), pp. 212–13.

4 *Séraphita* is a novel by Balzac, first published in serial form in 1834, in which the central figure—Séraphitüs/Séraphita—is androgynous. [Trans.].

ROLAND BARTHES

This will be borne home to us if we remember that the entire novella is structured around an initial antithesis which sets its symbolic level in place from the outset.[5] This antithesis is established by the narrator whose function is hence both rhetorical and anecdotal: as master of the discourse and of the story—of the story as discourse—he is the only one to be on both sides of the metaphor, to occupy the border between the two scenes. Like the poet, he has the whole paradigm in his possession—his body itself simultaneously bears witness to division and to relationship: half-hidden by a curtain as he stands in the window, one leg is chilled by the cold outside while the other feels the warmth emanating from the salon. The antithesis is actually between the garden lying dead beneath the snow and the brilliant party going on inside, bubbling with life. On the one side, the cold, the skeletal scrawniness of the trees, the whitish grey of the nocturnal clouds; on the other, the light, the heat, the dancing and the beautiful women, all associated with plant-related images of life that is at once full, rugged, powerful, mellow and fresh. This

---

5 In some cases, a narrative seems formally to develop a rhetorical figure, which serves more or less as its matrix. In *Sarrasine*, that figure is an antithesis. In *A Passion in the Desert*, it is a metaphor (the panther is a woman). In *La Mandragore* by Frédéric La Motte-Fouqué, it is an antiphrasis (managing to sell more cheaply than one bought). These are basic patterns and a typology of them may some day be attempted.

antithesis fuels the entire prologue, in which the contrast between castrato/death and woman/life is constantly being asserted. It might even be said that the prologue exists only to represent the two elements paradoxically alongside each other: it comes to a head when, by a curious aberration, the beautiful Mme de Rochefide is unable to prevent herself from *touching* the old man, thus causing a sort of paradigmatic conflagration, an explosion of antipathic substances. In the best traditions of poetic physics, these substances are, basically, cold (the tarnished, the motionless, the ossified, the bluish and the glaucous) and heat (the brilliant, the diaphanous and the perfumed). The aged Zambinella is absolute cold; the young Zambinella the mystification of a deep coldness concealed by a fresh, warm exterior. As a constant allegory has it (as though poetry in our country comes only from the North), the opposition between cold and hot is none other than the opposition between creativity and sterility (without it being possible to decide which one 'comes first').

Art, which is also the subject of *Sarrasine* (there are many ways in to this novella), produces two allegories in the book: the allegory of the picture of Adonis (in the prologue), and that of the statue (in the story). In formal terms, art consists in an operation of gathering together. Over against his art, Sarrasine's real world is divided. It partakes of a major form of guilt, the guilt that attaches to the *composite*. Sarrasine himself is composite; he is 'by turns active or passive' (this is what

Romanticism, at least the Romanticism of Balzac and Michelet, calls 'the bizarre'). In Filippo, the castrato's great-nephew, despite his great beauty, we discover a mix of contrary elements (his slenderness and fine figure; his vigorous eyebrows and male passion). His mother and his sister, the one dazzling, the other gentle, have to be two different persons to fulfil an image of total woman. And before he encountered Zambinella, when Sarrasine was looking for a model for his sculptures, he could find only perfect *details* from various bodies: here, 'the roundedness of a perfect leg', there 'the curve of a breast', 'some girl's neck, some woman's hands, and some child's smooth knees' [238]. Confronted with this dispersion, art is that power which accomplishes the 'inconceivable conjunction' (as Machiavelli puts it when he sketches the portrait of Lorenzo de' Medici[6]): art alone can reassemble the

6 In the French text, Barthes cites the phrase 'l'inconcevable jointure' from the French translation of Machiavelli's *History of Florence*. Machiavelli actually wrote that there were, in the character of Lorenzo, 'due persone diverse, quasi con impossibile congiunzione congiunte' (*Istorie fiorentine*. Milan: Feltrinelli Editore, 1962, p. 576). The translation published by the Universal Classics Library (New York and London: W. Walter Dunne, 1901) renders this as 'will find united in him dispositions which seem almost incompatible with each other.' It will be evident that the quasi or almost has fallen out of the French translation. [Trans.]

body fragmented by fantasy (and, in this sense, art is a counter-fantasy).[7] For Sarrasine, Zambinella is an art object—is the very object of art—because his body brings together perfections which admittedly exist in various parts of the real but do so divorced from one another. Zambinella's femininity stems from 'her' perfection but 'her' perfection stems from her unity. What Zambinella impresses on Sarrasine the first time he sees her, is the truth of unity: the divided, creaking artist (as his biography informs us) finds himself suddenly—in a surprising description—'*lubricated*'.[8]

The relations tying Zambinella to the work of art are contradictory, or we have at least to analyse them without taking account of the succession of the episodes, since the end of a story cannot be taken to represent its truth. Taking a first view—the prosaic moment—the relationship is relatively simple. By chance, Sarrasine at last discovers in Zambinella the perfect model of the total statue he has always dreamt of: working from memory, he feverishly makes

[7] On the fragmented body in *Sarrasine*, see Jean Reboul's excellent study 'Sarrasine ou la castration personnifiée', *Cahiers pour l'Analyse* 7 (March–April 1967): 91–6.

[8] By contrast with painting, and even more with sculpture (it is not for nothing that Sarrasine is a sculptor), writing cannot gather the body together; it is condemned to a succession of details: language cannot provide beauty but only its cipher.

ROLAND BARTHES

sketches of her, drawing her in every pose and, in that way, already confusing object and image, since his drawings are so many fantasies in which he makes of the woman what he wants, 'in short . . . sampling the future with her' [240] (the French word *avenir* is a profound one here that clearly denotes that future in which all fantasies are gathered).

At a second stage—the pathetic moment—as the fleshly model is deciphered and the castrato (the *nothing*) appears beneath the woman, art collapses, creation becomes impossible and the creator finds himself metonymically castrated ('You have dragged me down to your level' [252]). Sarrasine throws his hammer at the statue (though he fails to hit it) and dies. This is the moment of realist art, for in it the success of the work is entirely subject to the physical, material nature of the model: when the referent reveals its debasement, the sign itself is ruined. According to this conception, in order to produce a perfect work, the model, in its tyranny over the artist, must be known completely— including even its 'underside'. It isn't the outward appearance but the (organic) 'reality' of the model that underwrites the work. Biographically (but not, perhaps, symbolically), Sarrasine is a realist artist, for if the work is not in keeping with the secret truth of the model, it is a lie. The statue is good only if it copies what we cannot see of the woman. In other words, the work of art must have a reverse side; the folds of clay enwrap a woman whom we must be able to undress.

However, taking a third view, drawing on traces found in the anecdote, though they do not constitute its argument, the work of art and la Zambinella coincide exhaustively: there is nothing left over from the one in the other, and there is no risk of the physicality of the latter ever undermining the ideality of the former, insofar as both are, equally, imitations of Woman; it is very precisely because la Zambinella is a fake woman—or, more exactly, an imitation woman—that she is fully a work of art ('This was more than a woman, this was a masterpiece!'). Paradoxically, it follows that what Sarrasine loves in Zambinella is precisely castration, the precondition, at the level of the anecdote, for imitated femininity: his illusion is, to some degree, controlled by his nature as an artist ('Do you think you can deceive an artist's eye?' he says to Zambinella, who is trying to bring him back to 'reality'). In this way he comes, unwittingly, to recognize the *fitting* (if not *true*) concordance between Zambinella's perfection and the lack that constitutes her ('That angelic voice ... would be an anomaly coming from any body but yours').[9] Thus the whole novella brings out what we might call

[9] From the standpoint of a psychological analysis—though that isn't the standpoint of this study—it would be easy to show that what Sarrasine loves in Zambinella is castration itself; in that case, his aggressiveness towards what he believes, nonetheless, to be a woman would be noted, as would his insistence on declaring that what he loved

ROLAND BARTHES

the dialectic of Pygmalion (a theme expressly cited by the sculptor) which, for the artist, consists in loving the illusion itself, not its content, and defining his creation not so much by the fullness of its reference as by the divergence of its reflection. For to imitate is, ultimately, to defer. It is to put off reference to infinity. It is constantly to bring the 'depths' of the work to its surface. Works of art have no underside and it is in that respect that la Zambinella, in her way, was a perfect work of art: beneath *the dazzlingly white covering of lace that concealed her bosom* [243],[10] there was nothing less or nothing more than one could find beneath the varnish of the Adonis painted by Vien. We might say that the statue, which has about it a depth that can be probed, draws the sculptor into the passion for decipherment and brings the truth of the referent into play, whereas the painting (made by another, we should not forget), being immediate and without depth, without an underside and a core, holds the artist to the truth of illusion. As a painter, Sarrasine would not have tried to turn the canvas around and would not have been

in Zambinella was what made 'her' a castrato ('oh, soft, frail creature, how could you be otherwise?') and even the very femininity of that name Sarrasine, chosen against the masculine form, Sarrazin, commonly attested in French onomastics.

10 I have, in this case, departed from the translation in S/Z (p. 243), in order to stay closer to the French word order. [Trans.]

in danger of making the horrified discovery of the *nothing* underlying it. The Adonis painted by Vien from the statue that was saved from Sarrasine's destructive hammer, without the painter having ever seen the model, is something like a redeemed version of it: it nostalgically shows the artist the happy path of an art whose underside must never be sought out. Sarrasine dies from the belief that art is realist.

In Indo-European, we are told, the masculine or feminine character of a noun was not discernible from the noun itself but only from the masculine or feminine form of its adjective—from the standpoint of linguistic morphology, sex is only ever an attribute. Similarly, confronted with the very question from which he will die (is Zambinella a woman or not?), Sarrasine provides—and finds—only attributive proofs: the feminine character of la Zambinella, of which he is continually convincing himself, is, for him, only predicative. These proofs are of three kinds. The first kind derives from a state of affairs of which physical appearance is merely the mediation: beauty, which is a decisive proof of womanhood—what is beautiful can only be feminine ('He is too beautiful for a man,' says Mme de Rochefide of Vien's Adonis [232]). Being of superlative beauty, la Zambinella can only be a super-essential woman (the beauty of young Filippo is noted only because it also has about it something of the graceful fragility of the singer). The second kind of proof, more important because it comes in at the most dramatic point, and more decisive since it upholds Sarrasine's conviction despite Zambinella's own avowal, is the psychological: Zambinella can only be a woman because she possesses to an absolute degree the characterial nature of woman—weakness. The more deeply involved in the adventure Sarrasine becomes—and the more the risks of deciphering Zambinella's sex increase as a result—the greater the importance that character's weakness assumes in Sarrasine's eyes. It bolsters his blindness. The weakness is at first merely touching, it is part of Zambinella's charm; it subsequently becomes essential, serving to define at a stroke both genus and species, women and la Zambinella ('This was woman herself, with her sudden fears' [248]). Sarrasine is on the look-out for any faintheartedness on Zambinella's part since it is *proof* to him of womanhood, being the specific feature of the gender ('Now do you dare deny you are a woman?' says the sculptor to Zambinella, who has been frightened by a grass snake [248]). The more difficult it becomes for Sarrasine to maintain his conviction and the more a crisis threatens, the more emphatic does Zambinella's weakness become. It is therefore logical—though the effect of this is paradoxical—that, as the truth emerges, Sarrasine makes a last effort to rescue the woman from the castrato, loading upon her such an atrocious weakness—cowardice—that she cannot in any way share it with him. When Zambinella collapses under the sculptor's violence, he shouts out: '"Ah, you are a woman, ... for even a ..." He broke off' [251], which means that in Sarrasine's eyes even a castrato would not be so cowardly. At this point, Zambinella's weakness is no longer merely negative, for, in terms of the verisimilar register, it serves to prove femininity, but in terms of the discursive register, it attaches specifically to the castrato as that different *sameness* that founds all imitation. Thus Sarrasine can confess without contradiction that it is precisely this excessive weakness he loves about Zambinella ("'Explain to me," he said, "how this extreme weakness, which I would find hideous in any other woman ... pleases and charms me in you?"' [248]): paradoxically, it forearms him against the wiles of inversion, which can always put a little bit of the male in the female ("'I think I would detest a strong woman, a Sappho, a courageous creature, full of energy and passion"' [249]). There is, lastly, a third proof of Zambinella's femininity, just as attributive as the first two, and this is Sarrasine's passion: what is designated as an object by men can only be a woman. In terms of the argument, Sarrasine's passion is two-pronged and paradoxical, since it is directed towards a male, even a castrated one. But in terms of the discourse, expressed in signs of violence, joy and protection and in acts of amorous transport (devouring with his eyes, planning an abduction, etc.), it is, by contrast, continuing proof of Zambinella's femininity. Thus *proof* for Sarrasine is, indeed, of a rhetorical kind: the reasoning he follows is no other than the *argumentum* of the ancient rhetoricians. In other words, it is an approximative syllogism or enthymeme, based on a premise that is merely verisimilar: woman is beautiful, weak and loveable, says Sarrasine; Zambinella is beautiful, weak and loveable; therefore Zambinella is a woman. And the purer these qualities are in her, the more she fulfils the super-essence of Woman.

However, refracted on to the surface of discourse, the problem of proof is quite different: at this level, the index of femininity—or its mask—can only be gram-matical. The entire novella runs up against the con-straints of language, for, in speaking of the sopranist, a decision has to be made about which pronoun to use: masculine, feminine or neuter (if such a thing exists)? Admittedly, if Sarrasine were telling his own story himself as he was living it (that is to say, without knowing the end in advance), he would simply have to refer to la Zambinella on every occasion by an explic-itly feminine designation. The narrator, however, has other obligations: he has to work within the con-straints of suspense (and, consequently, resort to the feminine of illusion: she moved forward, she smiled, she is afraid, etc.) and yet, to keep the lying to a min-imum, so to speak, for it is a requirement of discursive verisimilitude that the narrator, being godlike and omniscient, cannot stoop to positively falsifying his statements. At the very most, he can lie by preterition. Hence the narrator is confronted with a generalized syllepsis, since he has to decide at every point whether to write in a way that conforms to meaning or to grammar. The Balzacian narrator solves this problem by following the 'mind' of his protagonist as closely as possible: Zambinella is feminized while Sarrasine believes him to be a woman; she becomes a 'he' when the *musico* is unmasked. Thus, the Italianism that makes it possible explicitly to feminize proper names (*la* Zambinella) disappears with the illusion of womanhood: the text then refers, simply, to Zambinella ('Zambinella, having recovered *himself*...' [250]).

Things become complicated because it isn't possible in a text to distinguish exhaustively and thoroughly between character, narrator and author. There is a level of all writing where one cannot decide *who is speaking*. 'This was woman herself, with her sudden fears, her irrational whims, her instinctive worries, her impetuous boldness, her fussings, and her delicious sensibility' we read at a certain point. Who is saying this— Sarrasine, the narrator, Balzac, universal wisdom, romantic psychology? No answer to this question will ever come: like Vien's Adonis, writing has no underside and we would seek in vain to turn it around to see 'what there is behind it'. Something is speaking here that is simply like the *obliqueness* of every subject. Signs of exteriority are, therefore, inevitably scattered here and there, not out of respect for the hidden truth but in order to fulfil the more or less germinative nature of every narrative tissue or, more precisely here, the requirements of suspense, which demand that the reader should be constantly alerted to the very signs of the code (in the sense of cipher). This occurs primarily in *Sarrasine* through the recourse to a number of substitutes for the neuter. The neuter is actually impossible in French. Even if it were possible grammatically, it would nonetheless be dangerous discursively, for it would either unmask the castrato too soon (neither man nor woman; we have seen that in our mythology the neuter is felt as desexualization and not as de-animation) or it would denote the desire not to choose between the two sexes, which would already be to say too much. The narrator can only index the castrato discreetly, by what we might call the feminine neuter ('such a charming creature', a 'feminine organization'). It is, subsequently, some very fleeting marks of the masculine, which, though they pass quickly in the discourse, nevertheless impress a sort of oscillation on the opposition of the sexes ('Je puis être *un ami dévoué* [masculine] pour vous, dit *la Zambinella* [feminine]'; 'I can be your devoted friend' [247]), as though, having no possible recourse to a morphological neuter form (as a result of the constraints of the language), it were nonetheless hinted at by keeping two opposites dangling.

There is a moment at which this acrobatics of marks reaches its outer limit (a moment we would be tempted to see—a little solemnly—as the truth of literature) and this is the point when the mark becomes purely graphic. If, from the standpoint of verisimilitude, every use of 'he' or 'she', when we imagine it in abstract terms, can still pass for indirect discourse (that's how Sarrasine would speak, the narrator seems to be implying), this fiction collapses, at certain points, when it has to be written down. 'Je vous ai semblé *jolie*', says Zambinella ('I seemed pretty to you' [246]; the adjective *jolie* is feminine): the narrator has to lie along with the castrato. As the most artificial form in the language, the agreement of the past participle imposes an implacable restriction and closes off all possibility of preterition. The narrator may play on a kind of circulation of minds and words, but the sculptor is up against the obligatory conventions of the graphic language—his only possible resort is to a systematic truth, irreducible to any other, which is the truth not of the author but of writing.